WHAT ON EARTH

HAVE I DONE?

Also by Robert Fulghum

WHAT ON EARTH
HAVE I DONE?

*Stories, Observations,
and Affirmations*

Robert Fulghum

St. Martin's Press

NEW YORK

www.stmartins.com

Library of Congress Cataloging-in-Publication Data

Fulghum, Robert.
    What on earth have I done? : stories, observations, and affirmations / Robert Fulghum.—1st ed.
        p. cm.
    ISBN-13: 978-0-312-36549-3
    ISBN-10: 0-312-36549-7
    1. Life.   2. Fulghum, Robert.   I. Title.

BD431.F875 2007
814'.54—dc22

                                        2007020487

First Edition: September 2007

10   9   8   7   6   5   4   3   2   1

Questions asked of children by parents:

"What on earth have you done?"
"What in the name of God are you doing?"
"What will you think of next?"
"Who do you think you are?"

Questions I still ask myself:

"What on earth have I done?"
"What in the name of God am I doing?"
"What will I think of next?"
"Who do I think I am?"

WHAT ON EARTH
HAVE I DONE?

Mother Questions

My house in Seattle is across the street from an elementary school. A high fence blocks my view, but I'm close enough to overhear conversations. One morning I was out in my yard at the hour when children were being delivered to school. I heard a car door opened, then slammed shut: *KABOOM!* Another door was opened, and a woman's voice came blasting over the fence:

"BILLY ... WHAT ... ON ... EARTH ... HAVE ...
YOU ... DONE?"
"Naaannggnnhhh ... ," wailed Billy-in-the-backseat.

What on earth had Billy done?
Maybe spilled a whole bottle of apple juice or opened his lunch bucket and spread the contents around looking for the cookies.
Or, worse, he had quietly vomited his breakfast all over

himself and had taken off most of his clothes. Or picked a scab until blood flowed.

Or used a plastic picnic fork to tattoo his name into the back of his mother's seat. Or decorated the upholstery and himself with a red magic marker his mother didn't know he possessed.

Having played both starring roles in this small domestic comedy in my time, I can attest to the possibility that the kid had accomplished *all* of these moves during the short trip from home to school.

My own mother asked me the same question. Often. And I, in my turn, asked my own children, who, no doubt, have followed the same line of inquiry with their kids.

"WHAT ON EARTH HAVE YOU DONE?"
This is one of the great Mother Questions.
The second great question mothers ask is the theological
    one:
"WHAT IN THE NAME OF GOD ARE YOU
    DOING?"
Another Mother Question anticipates the future:
"AND WHAT WILL YOU THINK OF NEXT?"
(My father rolled all these questions into one—only the
    tone changed:
"WHAT THE HELL . . . ?")

Children know these questions have no reasonable answers. Any child who has half a brain will go mute or mumble, *"Nothing. Nothing."* Or resort to pity-invoking sobs that plead innocence, ignorance, and helplessness:

"*I don't know* (snork) *I don't know* (snork) . . ."

And the child is telling the truth.

Most of the time a kid doesn't think about what he's doing, or why.

This is the privilege of childhood.

Now, at a distance from childhood and parenting, I begin to understand that these Great Mother Questions are, in fact, profound. They are the great Life Questions. Questions of accountability.

Muttering under my breath after yet another screw up, I echo both my mother and father: "What on earth have I done . . . what the hell . . . ?"

When asked of one's self in a calmer spirit, this line of inquiry makes sense, provokes thought, and even puts my feet back on the right path.

For example: "Well, just what on earth have you done?" After all these years—what? I think it's useful to inquire of myself about the quality of my existence and my contribution to the commonweal. Never mind what I set out to do. What have I done? What's my record as a citizen of Earth?

Likewise, "What, in the name of God, am I doing?" queries my actions on behalf of all that I say I believe and hold sacred.

And, finally, the question with ongoing relevance: "What will I think of next?" is a way of asking if my mind is a stagnant cesspool of worn-out notions or if I am mentally active—still replacing archaic information with fresh and better ideas? Am I still thinking—still asking—still learning?

When my mother asked me her questions I hated her.

Her tone of contempt raised blisters on my soul.

Looking back now, what I really hated was knowing that there were no acceptable responses to her inquest. This was not an invitation to a friendly symposium. She wasn't really asking. She was obliquely declaring that I was a loser, an idiot, and a pain in the ass.

I suppose I was, at least some of the time.

But, then, so was she. Some of the time.

Now I think better of her. And me. And the questions.

So. Energized by my thinking, I hurried around the fence to enlighten the mother who had been whipsawing Billy-in-the-backseat. The kid was gone. The mother was sitting in the car weeping and beating both hands on the steering wheel while muttering to herself.

I remember those parental moments. And this was not the time for the Unknown Wise Man to appear and explain to this vexed lady the deeper meaning of the Mother Questions.

I didn't want to have to answer that other great Mother Question:

"WHO DO YOU THINK YOU ARE?"

That's the big one, isn't it?

A flourishing life depends on how you answer that.

Who do I think I am?

The incontestable truth is that we come and go in sealed solitude. You cannot ever know what other people really think of you. Even your mother did not tell you the truth all the time. And the world will tell you what it thinks you want to hear, not always what you need to know.

What you think of you is what finally matters. When you look in the bathroom mirror in the morning, the court is open for business. And you are the jury and the judge on the case.

"Will the defendant please answer the Mother Questions:

"What on earth have you done?"
"What in the name of God are you doing?"
"What will you think of next?"

And if you know, you can say who you think you are.

2

Solitude

Thoreau's line is often quoted:

"The man who goes each day to the village to hear the latest news has not heard from himself in a long time."

As if solitude were a rare condition avoided by most people.

But the contrary is true: The man who hears only from himself most of the time, needs to get in touch with the village. Even Henry knew that. He didn't go very far and wasn't gone very long. And historians have proved that Thoreau walked the two miles into Concord almost every day, and he welcomed visitors at the pond.

Henry was lonely. That's why he finally moved back to town.

Solitude is our norm. And it's often as painful as it is pleasurable, especially if you are depressed or afraid or anguished or confused. Nobody is excluded from feeling left out.

The solution to alone-ness is not more solitude, but companionship and community. And to make inevitable solitude work in your favor.

If you want meaningful solitude, it's not far away, actually. Retreating to the woods alone isn't required. In shutting off phones, TV, newspapers, radio, and e-mail, and spending a day inside by myself without background distractions, I often hear from myself.

Sometimes what I hear is good news, but not always. Solitude is hardly guaranteed bliss. Onstage, in the theater of my head, is a noisy company of characters with contradictory opinions and quarrelsome tendencies. One is never really alone, because the play in one's brain is ongoing, and the clamor can be tiresome, whether you're asleep or awake.

"Who's in charge in there." I often wonder.

In another sense, when I am most alone, I am not alone, alone.

For example, in just an hour's walk this morning, I counted seventy-three people out by themselves—looking at the news of the day around them—thinking—hearing from themselves. Running, walking a dog, washing a car, or waiting for a bus. Some were out watering their flowers or tending their gardens, absorbed in their own inner process. We smiled, nodded, and acknowledged each other. Sometimes that is enough.

Solitude is not the same as loneliness.

Solitude is a solitary boat floating in a sea of possible companions.

Respect for mutual solitude is a requirement of society.

That's why Thoreau published *Walden*—to transcend solitude—to be alone but not lonely. He didn't keep what he thought to himself. He wrote it down and addressed it to other people in his books.

And that's why I write all these words to you—as a way of bringing the small boat of my life within speaking distance of yours.

Hello . . .

3

Intersection I

The following essays and stories are a continuation of an account of what on earth I've done, what I've thought of next, and who I think I am.

My own answers to the Mother Questions are provoked by the events of each day and sorted out in the solitude of my mind. Daily I feel I'm invited to the buffet of the world—a feast offered to the appetite of the imagination. The invitation says, "Help yourself." And so I have.

My best inclination says, "Share." And so I do.

Mine is a nomadic life now, seasonally moving between the city of Seattle, Washington, the La Sal Mountains of San Juan County, Utah; and the village of Kolymbari on the northwest coast of the Greek island of Crete. Thus geography frames the thoughts and tales.

Of course there are profound differences between these

cultural settings. But profound similarities, as well. Experience emphasizes that, way down deep, people and places are more alike than they are different.

One earth. One species.

Still, the apparent differences shine an enhancing light on what I might miss if I stayed in one place in a rut and never looked up at the scenery or stopped to watch the passing parade.

I try not to look back—that was then. And I try not to look too far ahead—that will come. I concentrate on looking around. Montaigne, who coined the word "essais" and refined the process of taking the ordinary seriously, remains my mentor.

Though edited into this book of stories, observations, and affirmations, the writing usually begins as journal entries— notes to myself—lines of verbal perspectives drawn from walking around and stopping at intersections as I move camp each year.

Often the raw ideas get molded into stories told to my longtime walking companion, Willy, who is probably unaware that for almost three decades he has been my real editor.

In time the stories and reflections migrate into book form. Even so, please keep in mind that I think of what I'm doing as writing letters and postcards to friends, always ending with the unspoken tag line:

"Wish you were here."

4

View Property

I moved. Keeping my small houseboat on Seattle's Lake Union as an office and place to write, I migrated to live in a house-house on Queen Anne Hill in a neighborhood of tree-shaded streets perfect for long walks. Proximity to an ice-cream parlor, a sports bar, a coffee house, a wine shop, bakery, barber, grocery store, and butcher shop were also part of the consideration.

Not long after I moved, a real estate agent asked if I was interested in selling my house. Remembering my father's dictum that, for the right price, everything he had was always for sale, I considered the matter and asked for a formal appraisal of the value of the property. Maybe I would move again.

When I heard the results, the figure seemed low. Less than I paid. *What? Why?* I asked what the market would consider to be the drawbacks of the house. What diminished its value? Answer: Location issues. A surprise to me, but here's what the report said:

"The house is across the street from an elementary school, which means noise and traffic during the day. The house is five blocks from a fire station, which often means noise and traffic in the middle of the night. And while the house is on the highest hill in Seattle, it really doesn't have much of a view. And view on Queen Anne Hill is everything."

Hmmm. The next day I timed my morning walk to coincide with the period just before the beginning of school, when the playground is full of children at play. I didn't hear their cacophony as noise, but rather as the jingle-jangle sounds of young life in full cry. I have three hundred young neighbors who are committed to learning—drawing, singing, dancing, writing, reading, math, and history—just to name a few items in their curriculum. And then there are their teachers with their talents and skills and commitments of their own. I see them come early and leave late.

It's hard to get better neighbors than that.

I say they *increase* the value of my house.

The school safety patrol is on duty at this hour, so I went to the corner to cross the street instead of jaywalking. A serious young man—fifth-grade caliber—asked me if I wished to cross. He's wearing an electric-green safety vest and carrying a red flag. "Wait, sir," he said with authority, "buses are coming." I waited—while a wave of nostalgia washed over me.

Once upon a time I was the captain of the West Junior High School Safety Patrol of Waco, Texas. A white, military Sam Brown belt, a military-style cap, and a red STOP flag completed the uniform. Five mornings a week, rain or shine, my unit lined up in formation on the school grounds for inspection, raised the American flag, and marched smartly around the school perimeter, dropping off squads of four boys at the corners. The last thing we did every afternoon was lower the flag. We felt important and useful. We were as serious about our responsibilities as the royal guards at Buckingham Palace.

"Sir, are you going to cross or not?"

The impatient fifth grader broke into my memory trance. He held up his hand. "Wait. Car coming." He looked both ways, boldly marched out into the street, held up his STOP flag, and motioned me on.

When he joined me on my side of the corner, I asked, "Why are you doing this, when you could be up on the school grounds playing basketball?" The look he gave me suggested he thought I was probably even older and more fuzzy-minded than I appeared. "I'm here to protect you, sir."

Of course. Protect me. I need that.

Five blocks away I passed the local fire station. Two firemen and a firewoman were out front polishing up the big red truck. I've had good feelings about fire stations and the people who work there ever since I was taken on a kindergarten field trip. I suspect that every child in America has had the same experience. The fire station is an educational institution. We take kids there as a way of saying that these people and what they do is good, important, and worthy of respect. They are exemplars. Be like them.

And modern-day firepeople are not at the fire station only in case something's burning. They're also emergency medics, trained to deal with injury and death. And they can handle hazardous-material spills and terrorist attacks as well.

I actually like hearing the truck roar by my house with its siren screaming in the middle of the night. It's the sound of safety. I sleep better knowing the firepeople are five blocks away, protecting me. I say it *adds* to the value of my house to know somebody will come running in a big hurry when the fruitcake hits the fan. I feel like cheering them on when they pass my house in the big red truck. Hurrah! Go get 'em!

Later, on the way back home, I walked by the fire station again. The truck was gone. I hadn't heard the siren, so I asked the one fireman I saw where the truck went. "Training session." Of course. All skills have to be practiced—all certifications renewed—all tool use updated. Their learning is ongoing and never ending.

When I walked by the elementary school again, all was quiet. Through the windows I could see the students at their desks—busy learning. I carefully crossed the street at the corner. I didn't want a patrol officer to look out the window and see me setting a bad example. I'd hate to be busted.

In my driveway I stopped to consider my morning walk and the real estate appraiser's evaluation of my house. How can it be said that I don't have all that much of a view? It is simply not true that you can't see much from my house.

Daily I view some of humanity's finest instincts: the desire to learn and know and serve. I can see firsthand the commitment to look after each other—the willingness to place one's self at risk for the sake of the common good. This is the essence of civil society.

My house is not for sale. I'm staying.

The view is priceless.

5

The Longer View

My new house was an old house. Built in 1906. And "just a little remodeling" turned into . . . need I go on? So I moved back out—into an apartment across the street—and the contractors moved into the old house. The most exciting part was the invasion of the company called "THE DESTRUCT DOGS." Five jolly three hundred-pound Samoan men with wrecking bars and sledge hammers. They even let me whack a few walls.

A major remodel of an old house in the city of Seattle requires an earthquake retrofit. And that involves an engineering analysis and a geologist's opinion. Serious business. We live in a zone where "The Big One" is long overdue. And there are occasional forewarnings. I was actually sitting in the living room of the old house planning the remodel when a small earthquake shook the city, so I'm a believer. Damage control usually involves bolting the house to the foundation with steel plates that run up into the second story. And I'm in favor of that.

The geologist came. I anxiously followed him around. When he was finished, he said, "There's good news. You are on the top of a hill that was left behind by two or three major glaciations over a period of thirty thousand years—the last one left just ten thousand years ago. Called the 'Vashon glacier,' it carved up this area coming and going. It was a tongue of a great ice sheet more than a mile thick, running from here all the way to Alaska."

He went on to explain that Queen Anne is a huge mound of cross-bedded layers of sand, gravel, rocks, clay, and soil. Where my house stands was covered by more than a thousand feet of ice. The weight packed all the loose rubble down nice and tight. In other words, my house sits on a superb shock absorber. The best place to be when "The Big One" comes.

"Is there any bad news?" I asked.

"Well, yes. The glaciers will be back."

"You mean . . . that someday . . . ?"

He gestured toward the surrounding city. "All of this. Someday. Scraped off and ground up and shoved into Puget Sound. We're in an interglacial age now. Just another phase of the cycle."

He laughed and went on to say that, unlike earthquakes, we'd have a lot of warning and could get out of the way. Geologist humor.

The long view.

The glaciers will be back.

And we . . . ?

6

Moon View

Here's a picture of several hundred people gathered on the high brow of Queen Anne Hill at dusk. A full Seattle cast, a marvelous mongrel mix of everything—old and young, male and female, white and black and brown and red and pink and freckled.

They're all staring in the same direction—a few are pointing. Almost all have an open-mouthed expression as if they are saying *"Oooooohhh"* at the same time.

It's the twenty-first century and the twenty-first day of July. What could possibly be astonishing enough to get them outside and so united in their attention? Explosions? Fireworks? A comet?

No, only this: The Magnificent Man in the Midsummer Moon has just lifted his orange eyebrows up over the rim of the Cascade Mountains. You can't see him in the photograph, but you can see him in the faces of all the people. *"Oooooohhh."*

———

"The Moon, the Moon, the Moon!"

And we're going back, or at least the planning is already underway at NASA. If the Chinese don't beat us to it.

It's heresy to say, but I'm not one who feels exalted by the first Moon landing, the orbiting space station, or the shuttle's yo-yo trips. Exciting? Yes. An indulgent diversion from reality? Yes. But that's about it.

The entire manned space program has not truly improved the quality of life on Earth, nor has it added anything of great value to the prospect of keeping Earth habitable and a happy place to be, which would seem to have priority.

Nor has it added one iota to the possibility that there is anyplace in space that is better for human beings than Earth. Superpower Pride was served and very little else. Ours is bigger and better than Yours is not a sign of advanced intelligence.

The Moon.

I liked it better when it was cheese.

However, on second thought . . .

There was a moment I wish the entire human race could have shared somehow. When astronaut Alan Shepard stood still on the surface of the Moon in 1971 and looked back at Earth, he wept. His tears came from see-ing the fragile beauty of home—this lovely, shining, blue and white ball floating in the vast darkness of space. So rare in its habitability for human beings.

"Gorgeous," he said.

And I wonder. How would it feel for all of us to be able to stand on the Moon on some amazing summer night and look back? Imagine that.

Staring, speechless, mouths open in amazement.

"Oooooooohh . . . ," we'd say.

"The Earth, the Earth, the Earth."

7

The Way It Has to Be

End of August. Downtown Seattle on a Saturday morning. Six young women carrying multiple shopping bags are standing in front of NIKETOWN. They are uniformly dressed in what an old grumpus like me thinks of as The Refugee Camp Look: Teeny-tiny T-shirts, bare midriffs exposing plump rolls of adolescent skin, worn and shredded skintight jeans that would better fit a little brother.

At the bottom of "the look" are the shoes, but not what I expected. The shoes are new, in a style I've not encountered before. Nikes? Oh, no. Clearly I'm a lap behind in the fashion race. All six girls are wearing brand-new, old-fashioned high-top canvas gym shoes in black, white, or red. The shoes are laced halfway, and the top half folded down into a cuff. No socks. The shoes are, they explain, "way, way cool. It's what everybody at school will wear."

Way, way cool, indeed!

"I haven't seen this style before. Whose idea was this?" I asked. "Did you come up with the shoe thing your-selves?"

They gave me blank looks.

"Well, like, you know, everybody knows. It just hap-pens."

"But somebody must have thought of it first. Where and how did you decide to go this route instead of what you were wearing when you left school last June?"

They didn't know. "It's just the way it has to be."

I would have given you the same line of thinking in late August of my senior year in high school when I had to have the mandatory outfit: a new, white, button-down dress shirt; some old farmer-boy overalls, and new, white buck suede shoes, which must be made as dirty as possible be-fore school starts. Haircut: flat top with a duck's ass in back. Way, way cool. The way it had to be.

Do not misunderstand. No pejorative intended. The eccentricities of the dress code of the young are always harmlessly amusing. Especially fifty years later.

Fashion fascinates me. It's the easily visible confirmation of how concepts and ideas move into, around, and out of the culture. Somewhere there is an Alpha Girl who first folded her canvas gym shoes' tops down. And somehow it caught on. And if my teenage shopper sample is accu-rate, in no time at all, this style statement will travel the world. And on the edge of the scene, the next fad is already coming.

Some truly deviant ideas get around, and prevail. It's not all just the fashion of the moment. Take just one example. This morning I put out three different garbage cans for pickup: one for glass, one for paper and plastic and aluminum, and one for disposable garbage. Recycling. Fifty years ago, I would not have known the word or understood the concept. *What? Are you kidding?* If asked, the young women I met could have told me all about recycling. They know. They do it. It's the way it has to be.

And did I mention the racial mix of my six young fashion consultants? Three White, two Black, one Asian. Fifty years ago they could not have gone shopping together or eaten together or gone back to school together. But now, it's the way it has to be.

I'm often pessimistic. Most of the incoming news of the world seems foully negative. And the smog of "same old, same old" stains my thinking. As an antidote, I look for any sign of any trend toward good news.

My early morning walk coincides with "Walk the Dog Time." This morning I counted eighty-three people walking ninety-one dogs. Every dog was on a leash. And every one of the dog owners—every single one—was carrying a plastic bag or some form of pooper-scooper. As unpleasant as the task seems to me, every time a dog dumped, their owner picked up after them. It still jars me a little when someone waves at me with a sack of poop held in the waving hand. I cannot remember the last time I saw dog poop left behind anywhere I walk. It didn't used to be that way. But it's the way it has to be.

Compared to larger human issues—war, famine, disease, cruelty, capital crime—controlling and cleaning up after pets is small potatoes. Yet here is one more readily observable proof that the habits of societies and the minds of people can change in favor of the common good. I repeat: It didn't used to be that way. I repeat: It's the way it has to be.

It's important to notice these things. Some good ideas get around and the world gets changed. I'm not always sure how or who sets it in motion, but there was a tipping point somewhere . . . somehow . . . someone. . . .

I know why, and it's not fashion:

It's the way it has to be.

8

Otters

The otters are gone. Good news. And sad news.

Backstory: My office and writing studio are in a houseboat on Lake Union in Seattle. (Houseboat here means, "Small old cottage built on a raft of huge cedar logs.") Despite the urban setting, we have raccoons, beavers, possums, and otters as part of the floating community, along with the usual ducks and geese and migrant water birds.

Live and let live. We like it this way.

Usually.

The otters, though shy and seldom seen, are sleek, graceful, and playful creatures. That's nice. But they crap a lot. An amazing lot. Not nice. And their toilet is the top of logs under my houseboat. Because otters eat fish and crawdads and clams, their feces really stink. Moreover, they like to pull out the insulation from under the house and make nests. When summer comes the smell is truly rancid.

And so. The otters had to go. First I tried repellant. Many kinds of repellant. Even coyote urine. The otters were unfazed. Then I was told if I saved my own morning pee and splashed it on the logs the otters would go away. Oh, sure.

But, out of desperation, I actually tried that. Employing a small porta-potty designed for boating, I hauled my own urine from home day after day. The otters were unfazed. The neighbors were unamused.

Next method: A high-pressure, motion-activated water jet. Though some kayakers were driven off with that one, the otters were not. Then I tried trapping the otters with humane catch-'em-alive traps. Caught three young inexperienced otters. And one small beaver. (Don't worry. All were taken away to live in the country.)

But the word got out in Otterland, and no matter what bait I used, no more were caught in the traps. All I got was more and more crap. Worse, now that winter was coming, the nest-building began. At night I heard them bedding down in my insulation. Happy sounds—like laughter.

Finally, I resorted to a two-wire, electric-shock fence around the perimeter of the houseboat, just above the waterline. Said fence, by the way, rearranged the prowling habits of several pussycats. (Cats can swim. Did you know that?) After several shrieks from unseen but clearly surprised otters, they packed up and moved on.

Victory is mine!

Maybe.

In truth, I feel bad about this.

First of all, the otters have probably only moved on to some neighbor's houseboat. Otters have been around a long time and can adapt to the situation. They'll no doubt be fine. And instead of a sense of triumph, I'm left with a hollow sense of regret. I haven't won.

Something lovely has gone out of my life. There's the image of otters running across a dusting of snow on my dock last winter, sliding on their chests into the water and coming around to do it again—clearly playing.

I remember the large and tiny tracks in the morning dew on my porch last spring—mother and babies. I remember seeing them floating on their backs out on the water while eating crayfish off their chests—the otter style of family picnic. To have creatures still living wild and free close by should be an honor.

I saw them as my problem.

But I am theirs.

And I am mine.

9

The Chair Men

We say the young have much to learn, but I find they know and do things unfamiliar to me, so I am pleased to learn from them when I can. Example: Two young college men asked me for a ride, because they were late to work. Their summer construction job was near my office, so I was glad to oblige. On the way I asked, "Besides working hard and playing hard, what's happening in your lives?"

They exchanged glances. Then one said. "We're eating a chair."

What?

Yes. It seems that their college philosophy teacher gave them an extra-credit assignment: Do something unique and memorable—not dangerous or foolish, but something creative, inventive, and instructive. Write it up, and explain what was learned and how it might apply to their philosophy of life.

So. They are eating a chair.

They bought a plain wooden kitchen chair at an unfinished furniture store. Using a wood rasp, they have been shaving away at the chair, mixing the dust into their granola for breakfast, and sprinkling the dust on their salads at dinner. So far they have consumed most of a leg, two rungs, and a back piece. And while they don't want to overdo it, the pace is picking up. Still, the project may not be finished before summer's end, so they may enlist friends, who, it seems, are enthusiastically willing to help eat a chair.

And yes, they consulted a physician to make sure the wood dust was not harmful. And no, it doesn't taste bad— especially if they mix in a little cinnamon at breakfast and a little lemon pepper at dinner. And yes, they have learned a few things along the way.

"Like what?" I asked.

Like how amazing long-term goals can be achieved in incremental stages. Like how something seemingly idiotic affects your thinking about other things you do. For example, they routinely run about fifteen miles a week to stay in shape—around and around a lake. They wondered where fifteen miles a week would take them if they ran in a straight line. So they got a road map and have been marking off the mileage, headed south. They could be in Portland, Oregon, in a couple of weeks. But that's boring, so they have a European map now and are starting out in Vienna headed for Athens. Using guidebooks, they're figuring out what there is to see and do along the way. They're touring the world in their minds.

And, of course, they're very pleased with themselves. They're sure they'll astound the professor when he asks for their report. "We ate a chair."

"It will blow the dude away," said one.

For all the goofiness of the project, these young men are learning patience and perseverance. Some things cannot be had except on a little-at-a-time, keep-the-long-goal-in-mind, stay-focused basis.

Love and friendship are like that. Marriage and parenthood, too. And peace and justice and social change. As wonderfully silly as it seems, eating a chair may lead my young college friends to wisdom and nobler aspirations.

In their foolishness lies the seed of What-Might-Be, little by little.

10

Watch Out for Trucks

A friend of mine, Brie, who was twelve at the time of this story, is willing to go anywhere with me that involves dressing up. She likes my company. I like hers. And we both like looking good and laughing hard. She's my kind of guy.

Technically speaking she is my grandchild, but I emphasize that we are friends out of mutual admiration, not merely blood kin. She is old and wise beyond her years. I am young and goofy behind my years. She aspires to adulthood but hasn't quite got the hang of it. And I know what's required of adults, but I just can't get used to being one.

With regard to dress-up occasions—one in particular: Brie went along with me to a wedding where I was the ministerial officiant. A very romantic occasion that went off much better than expected. Both the mother-of-the-bride and the mother-of-the-groom were perfectly pleased. Miraculous!

The bride and groom lived happily ever after—at least as long as the reception. Laughter, tears, hugging, dancing, eating, drinking. Whoopee!

A very lovey-lovey, kissy-kissy, happy-happy affair.

Home run with the bases loaded.

During the ride home, Brie was unusually quiet. I parked the car and we walked hand-in-hand toward my house, where she was spending the night. Still quiet. Suddenly she said:

"I wonder where he is tonight."

"Who?"

"You know—*Him*—the man I'll marry someday, the father of your great-grandchildren. He must be out there somewhere. Where is he?"

"I can't imagine. Why do you ask?"

"Well, I worry about him. . . . I hope he's OK."

"Well, if he's going to meet up with you somewhere down the road, then I'm sure he must be fine—safe in the hands of destiny."

(Silence.)

I looked down at her and saw trembling lips and teary eyes.

"What's wrong?"

"What if . . . he got hit . . . by a truck? . . . What if . . . he's hurt?"

I felt tears in my own eyes.

"That would be awful," I mumbled.

"Yes," she sobbed, "he will be so sad and lonely without me."

Just then we went through the kitchen door. My wife saw our distress.

"What's wrong with you two?" she asked.

"Her husband was hit by a truck," I moaned, "and we don't even know where he is or who's taking care of him."

"*What?*"

Somewhere out there in the world is a young man.

Him. The One Who. Mr. Someday. I have a message for him:

You don't know it, but something lovely will happen to you someday, whatever may be happening to you now. My dear friend, Brie, is on the way to you. Someday. When she gets there, you'll never be sad and lonely again.

When you meet her, she will be dressed up, looking good, and laughing. And if you are very, very lucky, she not only will become your wife, she will become your best friend. In the meantime, she and I think about you and worry about you. Please take care of yourself.

Watch out for trucks.

———

Underneath this story is the question I often ask myself:

"What will become of me?"

Somebody once asked me: "If you could know everything that will ever happen to you for the rest of your life, but you could not change a thing, would you want to know?"

Some days, yes. Mostly, no.

But I can't stop wondering, even if it makes no sense. Even if I don't really believe in Destiny or the One and Only. I wonder . . .

Meanwhile, the trucks of fate roll by.

The trick is to not get run over by one.

The trick is to be there, alert, by the side of the road, with your thumb out. So that if the truck with your number on it just happens to come along, you will know. And you will get in and go. And the ride will be as long and as lovely as you always imagined it might be.

11

Summer's End

Three tousle-haired and barefooted kids in the nine-or-ten-year-old class smile and wave from behind their lemonade stand on a corner not far from my house. They're very proud of their stand and especially their big sign:

FRESH COLD LEMONADE 25 CENTS.

Every word is spelled correctly and printed neatly. Being a sucker for lemonade stands, I stopped to sample their wares, and complimented them on the sign. "Well, we go to school, you know," said one, somewhat indignant that I would infer a lack of language skills.

They're doing a booming business, despite the fact that their lemonade is a bit sour. Part of their success is due to their father, supervising in a lawn chair from the shade of a tree several yards behind them. He has what looks like a small plastic water bottle in his hand. Checking to see if the coast is clear, he points to the bottle and flashes a large grin and a small sign at me. *"Shot of vodka, $1.00."*

Merchandizing is a subtle art.

On my way home from the lemonade stand I noted the traffic islands.

The city of Seattle has installed these round impediments in the middle of residential streets to slow drivers and keep neighborhoods from becoming alternate arterials to nearby road-rage routes. A few islands are dry and weedy and ugly by summer's end, but some have been turned into tiny botanical gardens by the people who live nearby.

I saw a lady directing traffic around the other side of an island while a man watered the plants from a hose connected to a hydrant at his house way across the street on the corner. The island has blue hydrangeas and orange nasturtiums and some tall, almost black African grasses.

The island itself doesn't slow the traffic. The beauty in it does.

Another island has two well-watered apple trees planted on it. The apples are greening into redness. A gray-haired

woman in a pale blue apron was checking the trees for insects and polishing the apples with a white dishcloth.

A block away is an island with several varieties of blue
and purple and white lavender completely covering it. I
can smell the perfume from across the street. Two children were carefully cutting stalks of lavender and putting
them in a vase.

These islands are public property, belonging to none,
available to all. Why bother to care for them? It seems
that some people think that the administrative staff of the
city of Seattle is not limited to the professionals who work
in city office buildings downtown.

Some people think that those who maintain the streets
for the city of Seattle are not just those who are paid to
drive around in uniforms in official trucks with official
equipment.

Like the girls on the school safety patrol, the island-
keepers have a larger view of what it means to take care of
their corner of the world. I stopped to thank one of the
island-keepers and admire the roses she grows in the public parking strip in front of her house.

A day later a bouquet of those roses appeared on my
front porch.

I write this on Labor Day weekend. How I hate it that summer is ending. Next week the rains will begin and most everybody moves their part of the street theater inside. The lemonade stand will be closed and the children back in school. And walking around in my neighborhood in the rain will be a lonely affair.

I will miss being so easily part of the community that summer provides. I will miss the many opportunities for the delight in what Thornton Wilder wrote about in his great play, *Our Town*.

He said the play was ". . . an attempt to find a value above all price for the smallest events in our daily life."

12

Cursed

A pair of black soccer shoes dangled from a power line way up in the air out in the middle of Bigelow Street near my house. I know how they got there because I was a witness.

Rained this morning. I was out walking in the late afternoon. Ahead of me by a block were four grade-school kids. Three sizes of boys and a gangly girl already taller than her mates. They were outfitted in team uniforms, headed home after practice. Three had their soccer shoes over their shoulders, tied together by the laces. One kid swung his shoes around and around and threw them up in the air. When they came down, he threw them up again. And again. Higher. Until they hit the power line and wrapped themselves around the line.

"OH-MY-GOD!" said one, clearly awed by the accomplishment.

"I can't believe you did that," said another.

The group stood and stared at the soccer shoes swaying gently above them. Then awe shifted to fear.

"Mother is going to kill you when she finds out," said the girl.

"His dad is going to beat the hell out of him," said another.

Everything must have looked so fine to Billy this afternoon. Fall. A new season. Hope for a championship and a trophy. New uniforms, new shoes, good practice, and school still a week away.

Now this. Death by Mother, beating by Father, banishment to his room, and no new shoes. He can hear it now:

"We are not going to buy you more shoes."

"Let that be a lesson to you. Don't do stupid things."

And no shoes means not playing on the team. And not playing on the team means humiliation. There will be all the "Ya-ya-ya-ya—Billy hung his shoes on a power line." Nothing like beginning a new school year and a new season as a loser.

Cursed.

Billy is desperate. "Don't tell. Promise."

"But that won't get your shoes back. And you'll have to lie."

"We could put a sharp knife on a long stick and cut them down."

"All we need is a big long ladder."

"It's a power line—we could get killed."

And so on, and so on and so on after that.

And then the Big Brilliant Idea strikes—an epiphany: Call 911.

This is an emergency situation, surely.

And those fire guys have big ladders and they get cats down all the time and they wouldn't want kids to mess with power lines and so maybe if they call 911 and tell their story the fire guys would come and meanwhile they could hide in the bushes and the fire guys would get the shoes down and just leave them on the sidewalk or something and nobody would ever know. Brilliant!

The girl got out her cell phone.

Sounded like a plan to me, but I didn't want to be included in it. I turned around and walked home. And I don't know exactly what happened, though I did hear a siren wailing after a while.

Probably wasn't the fire guys. More likely an ambulance carrying Billy's remains away after his father beat the hell out of him and his mother killed him and he died in humiliation and shame because he is such an idiot and a loser.

You know his sister didn't call 911.

Of course not.

She called her mom, who is, you will recall, Billy's mom as well.

And there went the season.

So young to have to bear a sports curse.

He'll never live it down.

Years and years and years from now, at every family gathering:

"Remember the time Billy hung his soccer shoes on the power line?"

"And tried to get me to call 911."

"Well, it might've worked."

"Right, Billy. Still an idiot."

Cursed.

13

Back and Forth and Back . . .

After a week of rain the skies cleared and the temperature warmed up, promising a spell of Indian Summer. Out walking, I stopped by the neighborhood playground where the best swings are. In summer, early and late, I usually have the swings all to myself, and I often sit and swing for a while. And so I have done this evening.

But I was not alone. Children were allowed back outside after supper to play in the fading light, and the playground rapidly filled up. Soon, all of the swings were occupied. A little boy marched up to stand in front of me.

He stared at me for a bit, and then said:

"I want to swing. You're not a kid."

"Yes, I am," I replied.

"No, you're not."

"Yes, I am."

"NO, YOU'RE NOT!" the kid shouted.

His father got up off a bench and walked over to see why his son is shouting at the white-bearded man on the swing. *Trouble.*

"What's wrong, Billy?"

"He won't let me swing. He says he's a kid."

The father considered me.

I, still swinging, considered the father.

The father smiled. Then laughed. Then turned to his son.

"He is a kid," the father explained. "Just a big old one."

"Thanks," I said.

The father took the son by the hand.

"You can wait your turn. Come teeter-totter with me."

And they did that.

It will be a long, long time before the kid is old enough to understand. Someday when he is a big old kid I wish for him the small joy of sitting in a swing in the soft September twilight. May he remember the example his father and I have set. And keep on swinging—back and forth and back and forth . . .

14

Used Feet

"Would you like to use my feet? My shoes are twelve inches long."

An offer I made to three girls across the street from me who were absorbed in measuring the distance from a sign to a parked truck. The girls were fifth graders—safety patrol members in charge of the elementary school crosswalk at the corner nearest my house.

"Yes," they shouted in chorus, and one of them raised her red STOP flag and escorted me safely over to the scene of a possible crime.

Here's the situation: A sign on a tall post on the corner says: NO PARKING WITHIN 30 FEET. A pickup truck with a construction company's logo on it is parked closer than the girls think it should be. The girls are empowered to report the license numbers of any vehicles breaking the law while they are on duty—usually those driving too fast or not stopping for children. It's been a slow morning, and the only opportunity for the girls to exercise their authority is this parked truck. And it is not an incidental issue. The truck does ever so slightly block their view of oncoming traffic.

What to do?

So I carefully walked the curb, foot-in-front-of-foot, from sign to pickup, and sure enough, the truck is twenty-seven feet away from the sign. Aha! Busted! One girl, the sergeant in charge, has her pad and pencil at the ready. Wait—not so fast—the girls are not in agreement.

What will happen to the guy if they turn him in? Will he be arrested and taken to jail? Is three feet over the line really such a crime? Does "thirty feet" mean exactly thirty feet or "somewhere around" thirty feet?

And there may be mitigating circumstances. "My mom does this all the time." "Maybe he's somebody's dad." "Maybe he'll be right back and we can talk to him." "Yeah, maybe just warn him about not doing it again."

"But the law is the law, and he's broken the law." "Yeah, but only by three feet." "Besides, it's almost time to go to class—maybe he'll be gone when we come back." "Does it really matter?"

They did not ask my advice. And I didn't want them to ask. On their own they were sorting out elementary issues of human community. That's why they are in elementary school. Underneath the specific issue lay the fundamental ones: What is right? What is wrong? What is the law? What is justice? And what part should mercy play in figuring the equation?

They were not leaving until they decided what to do.

But I quietly went my way—out of sight and, I hope, out of mind.

They were doing just fine by themselves. They didn't need me, only my big feet. And only then because they wanted to establish some objective facts. Good on them.

What did they decide? I don't know. They and the truck were gone when I came back. But I do know that how they were deciding was admirable—using their minds to figure out the right thing to do. They could have ignored the infraction and gone to class. But they knew their job and accepted the responsibility. I went on home feeling that their corner of the world was in very good hands.

All too soon they will confront conflicts around drug and alcohol use, sexual experience, women's health rights, and political leadership. I trust they will continue to do what they did this morning—get the facts and use their minds in a collaborative way in the name of justice. Make a judgment and act on it—knowing that it's never simple or easy.

If I could have said anything to them I would have pointed out that they, like the driver of the truck, were in the construction business—responsible for building and maintaining a just world, one small decision at a time. Taking good care of their corner.

And as to their question: "Does it matter?"

Yes, it matters a great deal.

15

Cheese Head Rules

Most men don't shop. They re-supply. They know what they need. They know exactly where it is—which store and which shelf—and they go in and get it and leave. No fooling around in the aisles. In—buy—out. That's it.

I am of these men.

The next morning, after aiding the safety patrol, I was on my way downtown. Need new socks. Twelve pairs—six black and six brown. Know exactly where they are. Annual trip to the men's shop in Nordstrom's emporium. Same as last year and the year before that.

Park. Move out. Street corner. Red light. No traffic coming in any direction that way or that way. No cops. Single-minded men on a sock resupply mission are exempt from stoplight rules. Red lights are for the children and old ladies. Go.

Five hurried steps into the street I notice a family

standing on the curb opposite me. All four are wearing
green T-shirts saying "CHEESE HEAD FROM WIS-
CONSIN" in big white letters. Tourists from a state that
has turned a pejorative nickname into a badge of pride—
meaning good-humored solid citizens: conservative, hard
working, law abiding, and proud of it.

The two girls and the mom and dad are holding hands
while patiently waiting for the light to change. The two
little girls—maybe nine and eleven years old—are staring
at me.

Or rather they are staring at a mature adult male citizen blatantly crossing the street against a red light. They
are probably Safety Patrol members—sisters-in-arms of
those three girls I had praised yesterday for taking care
of their corner of the world.

Time stood still. The light stayed red. The girls were
now pointing at me. The warning alarm in my head went
off: BEEP, BEEP, BEEP! My conscience starts muttering, *"Hypocrite, phony, charlatan."* Now the parents
are staring at me.

I am hating every moment of this situation.

Sigh. I stop. Turn around. Retreat to the curb. And
wait.

The light finally changes to green. The family from
Wisconsin and I begin crossing. And just as they pass me,
the oldest girl flashes a fine grin in my direction and gives
me the thumbs-up sign.

A gesture of mercy on a penitent.

We watch each other, you know. And often watch out for each other as well. I do not know the names of those girls or where they are now, and they may never know that I am telling you this story, but they were watching out for me and you and us.

Later, mission accomplished, I walked more thoughtfully back to my car. The red light event troubled me. I recalled the eighteenth-century French philosopher, Jean-Jacques Rousseau. In a philosophy class in college, I was exposed to his notion of the Social Contract. Most simply stated this is the implied agreement we make to live together in an orderly society. Without a covenant to abide by fundamental standards, anarchy results.

We codify these agreements into laws, but the laws depend on an attitude about the nature of community. That attitude is always on public display in respecting the simplest rules. For example, "Except for emergency vehicles, a red light means STOP. Always. For everybody. Period."

Elemental.

Why is it that I sometimes act like that rule doesn't apply to me?

The Mother Question echoes: *"Who do you think you are?"*

Answer: A cheese head. But not the kind from Wisconsin.

16

First Grade and
a Trilobite

Full Harvest Moon last night. If my feeble math skills serve me half well, I might have seen the moonrise about eight hundred times in my life, though I probably missed half of them because of weather or because I was too young to know what was going on. And I may have seen as many as thirty Harvest Moons. More than ever, as I age, I try to be there for the lovely moments, like the rising of the moon in the fall of the year.

Walking home, I passed the local elementary school and stopped to look into the window of a first-grade classroom, where the lights were still on as the janitor finished his work. I see that the first grade is through the "B's" now—"B is for bat and ball and bed and bird . . ." and so on. Also two big B's back to back make a butterfly, which can be turned into a work of art with crayons. "C" is coming. Along with addition and subtraction.

All the neat little desks and chairs, and workbooks, and

bins of games are there, ready for tomorrow. It's like looking into a dynamite storage room, knowing that, come
morning, the miners in the pit of learning will be back at
the seams of knowledge, blasting and digging and hauling
away.

I envy them.

These first graders learn all day, have sleepovers and
playdates and recess, and someone to tell them a story
at night and carry them to bed and tuck them in. Maybe
that's what extended care is like when you get old and feeble and stupid. One last chance at the lovely moments.

In my pocket as I walk is a trilobite, which I carry and
turn over in my fingers as a talisman. It's a fossil preserved
in black slate from life 530 million years ago, when nothing like us was around.

I sat still in the moonlight on the bench on the highest hill in my mind, held my trilobite in my hand, and
considered the long view. It's my "ant-in-Chicago" position. An ant will never comprehend Chicago. Never. But
sometimes the ant must have a vague sense that something astonishing is going on around it. Vibrations and
energy and change. As I do.

The long view—the Big Picture: what's the meaning
of it all?

I can't seem to let go of the wondering. That's a good
thing. But meanwhile, I may, like those first graders, give

my life meaning by throwing myself recklessly into it daily, as if something astonishing is happening and I am part of it.

It is and I am.

17

Hopelessly Confused Sometimes:
A Story with Four Parts
and No End

Part One

Between my office and my home there are several traffic intersections where people regularly stand with cardboard signs asking for help: *"Homeless." "Will Work For Food." "Viet Nam Vet With Aids." "Why Lie, Need a Beer." "Need A Ride. Anywhere But Here." "We All Need A Little Help Sometimes."* And the most inventive sign: *"Ninjas Killed My Family—Need Tae Kwan Do Lessons."*

One woman in particular has drawn my attention several times. She doesn't stand with her hand out. She sits on a green plastic bucket looking down at her hands. She doesn't look very needy either: young and pretty, neat and clean, and dressed in the refugee-style of most people her age.

The wording on her sign varies: *"Stranded." "Broke." "Pregnant." "Sick and Tired."* And this morning's message: *"Hopelessly Confused."* What to do for her? I don't know.

It's easy to excuse my concern for these intersection beggars by thinking most are probably not helpless—begging is just their day job. Some must be scam artists. And some may be addicts or drunks wanting only enough cash for a fix. And some are probably already on all kinds of welfare—many outreach programs are available in Seattle.

So I tell myself.

I've thought it through. Often.

But still, there I am, idling, waiting for the light.

And there they are, six feet away.

I have far more than enough. They do not.

And here we are, face-to-face.

Part Two

I wondered what it would be like to be out there on the street. I tried to imagine myself hunkered down on a corner, looking old, ugly, scruffy, and pitiful—with my *"Need Help"* sign. Just to feel what it must be like to do what they do.

I could imagine doing that. I just couldn't bring myself to actually *do* it. But maybe I could come close. So, on Friday afteroon, when I saw a street-side beggar, I parked

my car and stood in a bus-stop shelter about twenty feet
away and watched.

It was five o'clock, hot day, roaring traffic, cars with
people headed home from work. Raggedy middle-aged
guy with a sign: *"Homeless Viet Nam Vet."* A wave of rejec-
tion washed over him. People stared or looked once, then
pointedly looked away. A few changed lanes to avoid him.
One rolled down his window and shouted, "Get a job,
jackass!" Two guys in a van flipped him the finger, and a
car full of teenagers swerved at him and honked. In an
hour he got one smile and one dollar and one hell of a lot
of hostility. I felt bad for him and bad for the human race.
But not half as bad as he must have felt. A hard, miserable job. You would have to be both tough and desperate
to do it, no matter what your reasons.

So what happened next? I did what you would do.
Talked to him. Gave him twenty dollars and a ride back to
the shelter downtown where he spends the night. I didn't
feel like I deserved any credit. I could not fix his life. I
know that. And pity is not compassion. I know that. He
would be back on the street tomorrow. I know that, too.

Part Three

And how about that girl on the green bucket: *"Stranded,*
Homeless, Pregnant, Sick and Tired, and Hopelessly Con-

fused?" The combination of her appearance and her signs mystified me. Maybe she is really involved in research of some kind. Writing a Ph.D. thesis on homelessness. When I saw her again a few days later I parked, walked back, and said, "Hello."

She looked up and shouted

"I suppose you're looking for sex! Most guys like you are!"

What? How could she just glance at me and judge me?

"I only want to help," I said.

"Oh sure, they all say that. Well, I'm a drug addict with AIDS and you wouldn't want to screw me. Don't mess with me either—I've got a knife and I can protect myself. Just satisfy your middle-class conscience and give me some money and go away." (That's not exactly what she said. Her language was acidly crude.)

Her sign said: *"Hopelessly Confused."* And now there were two of us. And neither one of us was going to get any good feelings out of the encounter. Her cynicism and my naïveté didn't add up to a positive number. *Maybe she's crazy,* I thought. *But what difference does that make?* Before I could do anything, she picked up her belongings, crossed the street, and walked away, leaving only me on the corner.

I wished she had left me her sign. Hopelessly confused. That's me.

Part Four

These encounters with those who profess need will never be simple or easy or leave me satisfied, I suppose. And having tried, oh so briefly, to stand in the footsteps of those who ask, I am at least more convinced that they are all desperately needy if they are out there.

It is not my job to judge them. It is my job to judge me.

Sure, if I give something to each and all of them, I may in the process give to some who do not really deserve help. That's the chance I take, but I will have not missed anyone whose need is real.

I could do more. Right. And God and the government could do more. Right. Society could do more. Right. But never mind all that. In the meantime I am there at the existential intersection—in the moment—with more than I need. And they are there—in the moment—asking for help. And no matter what I do, I will go away feeling that nothing is finally resolved.

Maybe that's my problem: this matter of having something "finally resolved." Wanting to do good and feel good at the same time. Wanting a permanent, surgical solution when a temporary bandage is all that the moment requires. Having great expectations when a small kindness is enough. Hopelessly confusing a need to have a final YES or NO with the reality that only untidy MAYBE is ever possible.

I must not pass by—I cannot. Maybe being a bleeding heart is always better than having no heart at all.

18

Just a Moment

How many times in my life have I said that phrase?
Or, considering the phrase another way, how many
small moments of my life remain fixed in memory marking
sudden insight, epiphany, revelation, inspiration, enlighten-
ment, beauty, or joy. The sudden flash of light. The instant
of comprehension. So immediate, so evanescent.

There are those unforgettable big lightning strikes: Love
at first sight, comprehending algebra, flying solo, seeing your
mother as a person, and knowing that, this time, the jumper
cables are hooked up right. And so on.

But there are the small flashes—when time and again
something like a neutron of imagination collides with an
ordinary particle of perception in your senses and something
new and unforgettable flies off and sticks. And you were
glad you were there when it happened.

I know this is getting wooly minded. There isn't just the
right word for this experience—all the ones I know are too

small or too large. But I have no doubt you know what I'm talking about. Not the cosmic stuff.

Just a moment . . .

From time to time I will try sharing one of mine, beginning with a man and some rocks.

19

Rockman

Myrtle Edwards Park is a long, narrow strip of green on Seattle's west waterfront at Elliott Bay. The shoreline there is protected by a steep breakwater of granite rubble—gray, rough, angular stones of all sizes. Practical, but not pretty. Certainly not the raw material for art, unless you have the imagination of Rockman.

He makes sculptures out of those ugly rocks. Delicately balanced stacks of heavy jagged stones, four or five or even six feet tall. Not only do the piles seem to defy gravity, they seem to defy good judgment—because if a stack fell while he was working on it, he could get seriously hurt—toes or fingers crushed. Dangerous art. That's why people stand around silently, holding their breath while watching Rockman work.

He's young and homeless, part Mexican, part Black. Sleeps in the bushes at the park in a tiny tent. Started stacking rocks on impulse one afternoon. People stopped to watch and gave him money in appreciation of his skill and courage. Now this is what he does for a living. When he finishes a piece, he stands back from it and sings a song to it or recites a poem. Performance Art. At the end of each day, he lets people push the work over into the water. No problem. He values the process of making art, not the finished sculpture.

I wish I had a picture of Rockman to show you, but he asks that he not be photographed. His reasons vary. Says he's in the Witness Protection Program. Fears that one of his wives might recognize him. Claims that he is the love-child of Condoleeza Rice and the president of Mexico. Says that he is proof that aliens have landed and made a few mistakes.

You'll just have to imagine what Rockman and his art look like.

He has no problem imagining his life.

He has something I want but cannot have.

The memory of just a moment.

That particular magical moment that day when he looked at those rubbly rocks and saw . . . art.

20

Freaky

A tattoo convention was held this last weekend at the Fisher Pavilion at Seattle Center. Two hundred licensed professional tattooists displayed their designs and demonstrated their skills in open booths where actual tattooing and body piercing took place in full view of the conventioneers. Not exactly a WASP potluck supper.

In fact, I may have been a one-man minority. The crowd was young, multi-racial, multi-pierced, multi-tattooed and outlandishly dressed. And I was an older, white, clean-cut, bearded man in a jacket and tie, who was on his way out to dinner and had just stopped by to see what the counterculture was up to. They stared at me.

"Look at him—how freaky can you get?"

I did see a way for me to fit in sometime in the future. An elderly man in a black bikini bottom was posing for

photographers. His scrawny old hide was completely covered from neck to wrist and on down to his feet in traditional Japanese tattoos.

Cutie-pie young tattooed chicks with tight tank tops
and short shorts paid five bucks each to sit on his knees
to have their pictures taken with him.

Noticing me, he winked and said:

"Beats hell out of bingo at the nursing home."

21

Square

Not more than fifty yards away at the same time in the main court of Seattle Center, the free Friday-evening dance party was underway. Hearing the music as I left the tattoo convention, I wandered over.

Tonight it's square dancing, and there are several squares of older, experienced dancers hard at work. The women are dressed in low-heeled shoes with straps over the instep, with fluffy petticoats under colorful skirts. The men wear shirts that match the skirts. Now this is more like a WASP potluck.

They're an ill-built, odd-lot bunch of geezers, but damn, they can dance: so smooth, so easy, so together. The same with the couples' dances as well—waltzes, polkas, and two-steps. I might not give any of them a second glance in passing on the street, but I can't keep my eyes off them now.

One couple drew my attention. He was old and gray, and danced with the slightly awkward movements of a man with an artificial leg. I can see its outline underneath his trouser leg. She's old and plump and golden blonde. At the end of one arm is a steel hook, but she partners well while compensating only slightly for not having one hand.

What's their story? How did they lose their limbs? It doesn't seem to make any difference to them or their dancing. They're really good. They dance every dance. And laugh when they sit down. They seem very happy.

It's possible that they are.

22

Halloween Hangover

Only now, two days later, am I coming down from the sugar high of Halloween. Whatever well-meaning adults may say or wish, *IT IS THE CANDY,* stupid. Of course it rots your teeth and makes you fat and spoils your appetite and makes you manic and even sick. I don't care.

A three-day sweet-binge once a year is something to look forward to. Besides, my mother is not around now to supervise me. And it's not true that I'm a bad influence on my grandchildren. I do not eat candy around them because their mother is around. I take the candy surplus, as a favor to their parents, and eat it alone whenever I want.

These are the perks of seniority.

———

For Halloweening this year I wore my white-rabbit costume, with black mask, blinking red nose, fake blood running out of my mouth in which I wore fake fangs. And I moved along the dark streets in that baggy-pants rolling lurch perfected by young rapsters-in-the-hood.

Scary?

Questionable.

People were surprised to see the Easter Bunny at Halloween—especially the Big Bunny of Death. I figure even the Easter Bunny has a dark side. He's probably disappointed with his very limited role of hiding hard-boiled, dyed chicken eggs once a year. Big Deal. Being reproduced in chocolate so little kids can bite his head off can't make him happy with his job either.

Out in the night trick-or-treating with my grandchildren and nieces, I was suddenly accosted by an eight-year-old kid in a pig suit. "Stop!" he shouted. He peered at the Easter Bunny of Death with the white beard. "How old are you?" he wanted to know.

Busted by the Trick-or-Treat Police.

"Very old and very wicked. Did you know the Death Bunny eats little pigs?" I growled. He was not impressed. He shrugged his shoulders. There were much scarier things out on the sidewalk than an old guy in a rabbit suit.

Next year I want a two-humped camel outfit. Talking someone into driving the back end of the thing may be a problem. The Death Camel ought to freak out somebody.

Especially if he also stalks the streets at Christmas. Death Camels eat Wise Men. Did you know that?

Scary?

Questionable.

23

Flashlight Advice

Lots of flashlights out in the streets on Halloween. For safety, of course, but also because little kids really like flashlights.

It's an introduction to adult power. Toys but not-toys.

Longer lasting and less expensive than a lot of the junk we give them.

No fire, no smoke, no calories.

Just light—to shine in dark places.

Where there would be no light otherwise.

Not a bad metaphor for a basic life mission.

Not really kid stuff, after all.

If you want to please little children, give them their own flashlight.

Not cheapo, cutesy, throw-aways, either.

Give them real grown-up, heavy-duty rubberized flashlights.

With extra bulbs and batteries.

And show them all the neat things you can do with light.

Shadow figures. Monster faces. Tag games.

Remember?

Use your imagination. So they will use theirs.

The purpose of flashlights is to show the Way.

24

Fools and Fat Butts

A neighbor my age has resumed his childhood passion for bicycling. His new ride is a titanium-zirconium-carbon-fiber recumbent bike. Even with fifty gears, a GPS, and full shock absorbers, it probably weighs less than his laptop.

But it's not the bike that stuns me: it's his outfit. Cute red shoes, a *Star Wars* helmet that makes his head seem like it's going faster than the rest of his body, fighter-pilot sun goggles, and a color-splashed, skin-tight Lycra body-suit that leaves little to the imagination.

As I look at him, my steady grin is a ziplock on a belly laugh. I know the truth. He wants to look cool while reducing the size of his big fat butt.

He stopped by to decline my invitation to an evening of salsa dancing at my house. "Can't dance—I'd make a fool of myself on the floor," says he. Well, all right. But he doesn't mind dressing like a second-rate circus freak on a bike? When he rode off, I saw from behind his big fat butt looking like two loose cannonballs in a condom. No doubt he's never seen himself from this angle.

Well, so what? Most of us don't really know how we look from behind, even though tight-butt jeans are the fashion these days. Still, I didn't laugh. I admire his social courage on behalf of his health, though I wouldn't be caught dead in an outfit like his in public.

Too bad about his dancing phobia. But I can relate to that. The first time I went to a Cretan village wedding, I sat on the sidelines when the dancing began. I'm not Greek. I don't look or dress Greek. And the Greeks' fancy footwork intimidated me. *"Don't make a fool of yourself,"* I thought. Reading my mind, an older woman dropped out of the dance, sat down beside me, and said:

"If you do not join the dancing, you will feel foolish. If you dance, you will also feel foolish. So, why not dance? And I will tell you a secret: If you do not join the dance, we will know you are a fool. But if you dance, we will think well of you for trying. And if you dance badly to begin and we laugh, what is the sin in that? We all begin there. Come on."

I danced.

Why not dance the dance of fools, and laugh the fool's laugh, and wear the fool's outfit, and care less about how I impress others?

Worse than a fat butt is a fat head.

25

Thanksgiving Spring
for Babycakes

Out walking in the late fall afternoon, I am serving as a self-appointed inspector of the deciduous trees in my neighborhood. Making sure those trees that are supposed to be turning their leaves from green to yellow and orange and red are doing their job. And they are.

The northerly housekeeping gales have not yet blown through to sweep the trees clean. The leaves remain where they have fallen, which means the streets and sidewalks and lawns remain a many-colored carpet.

These long Seattle autumns take people by the hand, lead them out into a state of enchantment, and return them to sit quietly by a fire, sorting memories, preparing themselves for Thanksgiving.

Walking in that mood, I'm unexpectedly alarmed.

As I approach the neighborhood flower stand, I see buckets of tulips out on the sidewalk for sale. Tulips!

What's more, bowls of budding daffodils and narcissus are available. *What? SPRING? Now?*

"They're local," says the charming flower lady. "Forced in greenhouses. Between horticultural science and air express, you can have almost any flower you want any time of year. Seasons don't make any difference anymore. And since we're open twenty-four hours a day, three hundred and sixty-five days a year, you can have almost any flower you want anytime you want it." She explains this gently to me as if I have not yet been informed it is now the twenty-first century.

"But it's November!" I say, grumpily. "Autumn. Fall. Selling tulips and daffodils and narcissus now must be illegal or immoral or just plain wrong. Whose idea was this?!"

She smiles sweetly, and says I don't have to buy them or even look at them if the idea troubles me.

"Stay calm, Babycakes," she says, "It's OK."

(*Babycakes? Nobody ever called me Babycakes. Nice.*)

At that moment, a shaky old man walked slowly up to the stand. Hanging his cane on the counter's edge, he picked up a bowl of almost-blooming daffodils and said he'd take these—gift-wrapped, please. He explained to the flower lady and me how pleased he is to find the daffodils.

"My wife of fifty-seven years is dying in the hospital,"

he says. "She's ninety. Terminal cancer. A couple of weeks at best—a few days at worst. Last night she said how sad she was about not living long enough to see just one more spring. She's a gardener. Loves flowers. Loves spring. Wonderful to find these daffodils. Now I can give her spring for Thanksgiving."

Oh. Well, then . . .

"Babycakes will have a dozen tulips and a pot of daffodils . . ."

26

What Remains—a Letter
to Friends . . .

On the fourth Thursday night in November I went out walking around midnight. Overfilled with food and friendship after the feast of Thanksgiving, I was too wide awake and restless to turn toward my bed and sleep. Something was missing—a period at the end of the paragraph of the day.

The night was cold and rainy. The streets were empty of life. Venturing into a neighborhood off my usual path, I imagined I was in the coach of a slow and silent train passing through a village somewhere in Europe. All of the houses were dark and mysterious. Except the one on the corner.

A light was on in the kitchen. And I could see a woman washing dishes through a window steamed from the hot water in the sink. She wore a white apron over a bright yellow blouse. A striped dishtowel was draped across her shoulder, and from time to time she raised a damp hand to brush back a lock of gray hair from her forehead.

At first I thought she must have someone helping her, but then I realized she was alone, talking and perhaps singing to herself. Once she smiled, stopped, and looked up as if remembering something. She laughed and went on with her dishwashing. She, like I, must have had a splendid Thanksgiving.

When she was finished she turned off the kitchen light, walked into the dining room, came to a window, and looked out. It was raining hard now, but I still stood holding my umbrella under the corner streetlight, reluctant to let go of my momentary companion. She noticed me. She smiled and waved. I waved back. As I started to cross the street, I looked back. She was still there. *"Good night, whoever you are,"* I thought, *"And thanks for waving."*

I hope she wished me the same.

And I turned away as the slow silent train of my life moved on through the village of the world. Looking back one last time from a block away, I saw that the light in the living room was off. The house was dark.

This letter began the Sunday morning after Thanksgiving. Alone in the quiet of my house. Cold and stormy outside. Snow was falling at dawn, but not sticking—very slow rain. Slow is the operative word for the weekend. Bowl of oatmeal and cup of hot chocolate. Stay home. Go slow. Be still.

The dominant news on the radio was the tragedy in Iraq and the madness of holiday shopping. I caught the end of part of the president's saturday radio broadcast. "God Bless America," he said. I wish it was the tradition of those who represent us to the world to always say, "God bless everyone, everywhere."

I turned off the radio and turned away from the news of what I can't stop or fix. A long-distance call came from a friend in Greece. He began the conversation with a question. *"What the hell are you Americans thinking?"* I don't know. I don't know. I feel a sense of shame. Shame for what we're squandering in the world—the money, the good will, and peace. Shame for my complicity in the lies and stupidity and the dying. So I hung up and turned away and stared out the window at the falling snow. Be still. At least until Monday.

My mother-in-law died this week at eighty-six. Quietly, easily, softly, she went in her sleep after the long decline of Alzheimer's. Good woman. Second generation Japanese. A doctor—pediatrician. Faithful mother and wife. We placed her ashes in the family grave on Friday. She didn't belong to any religious community and asked that there be no service when she died. Thus, a small, simple quiet occasion. Only the close family members were present to say good-bye.

I had volunteered to pick up her ashes at the mortuary

and place them in an urn. The task was unexpectedly complicated. There was only a small hole in the bottom of the urn, and the only way to get the ashes inside was to pour them from the plastic bag through a funnel, which took some time and care.

An instructive experience, actually. A reminder of my own mortality. As I watched the gray, granular, sandlike remains slowly fill the urn, I considered the remains of my own life running through the hourglass of time. I try not to take death personally, but sometimes . . . sometimes, I do.

After the brief graveside service, I walked around in the cemetery alone after everyone else had gone. The image of that lady in the window on Thanksgiving night came back to me. A bright memory still. Sometimes it is enough to notice one another. For the time being, it's the best we can do.

To wave. To wave back. And go on.

When you read these words I hope you understand it is my way of waving to you. And I hope, with all my heart, that you wave back.

27

Sunday Morning

Sunday, Sunday morning. Some in church. Some in bed. Some in limbo. Some in slow motion to nowhere in particular. And one out alone looking for a small slice of the pie of delight:

Around 8:30, cool and foggy— shifting toward warm and sunny.

Walking along a quiet street, I hear a melodious voice sing out:

"Sweetie Pie; oh, Sweetie Pie; where are you, Sweetie Pie?"

I stop and listen. *"Who? Me?"*

The voice came from the porch of a house across the street.

Trees and bushes hide the front of the house.

All I can see are the bare legs of the woman who is calling.

Nice legs.

"Sweetie Pie; oh, Sweetie Pie. Where are you, Sweetie Pie?"

So, what the hell . . . what harm?

"I'm over here, darling," I answer in my best bedroom voice.

She can't see me either.

I'm hidden by the trees and bushes on my side of the street.

But she's hip and sings out:

"I hope you've taken your dump," she says. "Come eat your nibbles,"

Aha! A game is afoot.

"The dump is done. Can I have a latte with my nibbles?"

She doesn't back down.

"And would you like a tummy rub with that?"

She laughs.

I laugh back.

And now her shaggy little black dog has finished his dump and comes woofing across the lawn and charges up the steps.

"Come to momma," she says, "I didn't know you liked coffee."

I wander on down the street, and the lovely voice calls after me.

"Have a nice day, Sweetie Pie."

I see her now. An old lady in her nightgown waving from her porch.

Nice legs.

Nice, nimble mind, too. She's a player.

I walked on with the dog of my imagination running unleashed through the bushes of my brain, looking for a place to unload.

Too bad her dog came back.

I could have used a tummy rub.

28

Players

That Sunday Morning Lady is a Player.

Definition: Persons with enough nimbleness of mind to accept a surprise invitation to jump into a quick game of imagination. People with a loosey-goosey sense of mischief. Players are also Laughers. And you can't tell the Players by the way they appear on the outside.

Example: Here's a uniformed city bus driver standing in the door of his vehicle, staring into the rain. An invitation from me, passing by: "OK, here's the deal: I'll pay for the gas, and you'll drive us to California to the beach at Santa Monica."

With a straight face he says, "OK, meet me here at midnight. It's the end of my run and they won't miss me or the bus until morning. I'll get some barbecue." He smiles.

A Player.

Consider this lady with a shopping cart full of oddball stuff standing beside me in front of the cheese counter at the grocery story. My invitation: "I like the groceries in your cart better than mine. Want to trade? You take mine and I'll take yours. Could be interesting when we get home."

She smiles. Checks out my cart. "You've got a deal," she says. We take each other's carts and roll away.

Later, she's waiting for me at the check-out counter. She knows and I know: we weren't really going to go through with it. But those few moments of madness brought new meaning to "going to the store for a few things." And the lady knows the game.

A Player.

On the other hand: There's a tailor shop on Queen Anne Avenue. Sign in the window says ALTERATIONS AND REPAIRS FOR MEN AND WOMEN. The tailor is standing in the doorway. I stop. "I'd like to get altered and repaired," I say.

She looks at me cautiously. Goes inside. Closes the door.

Not a player.

Players may be discreet. Here's the charming woman who works at the sidewalk flower stand at a nearby market. She called me "Babycakes" just before Thanksgiving Day, but I haven't seen her since. Invitation: "Do I still look like Baby-cakes to you?" I ask.

She looks at me shrewdly. "Sir, it is the policy of the store that employees are not to get familiar with cus-tomers." "Oh, too bad," say I. She's no longer a player. As I turn my back and walk away, she whispers, *"Thanks for coming by, Babycakes."*

She's an undercover Player now.

Here's me again, at a well-known company to pick up copies of a manuscript. I am visibly annoyed—this is my third trip to get what was promised yesterday. The anx-ious clerk, Miss Saucer-eyes, is obviously new to the herd behind the counter and doesn't know what to do with me or for me. The work is still not done, despite prom-ises. Getting mad won't help.

"OK, I won't make any trouble," I say, "Just give me a really clever, off-the-wall creative excuse—the wildest thing you can think of. Make me laugh and I'll go away."

Miss Saucer-eyes is mute. This situation was not cov-ered in training school last week. "I'll speak to my man-ager."

Definitely not a Player. But the story continues.

Miss Saucer-eyes retreats to the back of the shop and consults with her boss, a high-energy, sharply dressed woman, who marches briskly toward me with a steely look. She leans over the counter and explains:

"Sir, you may not know this, but this store has been a front for the Irish Republican Army for years. We're supposed to be turning in our firearms, and it seems a bazooka is missing from the inventory. When we find the bazooka, things will get back to normal. If I were you, I wouldn't make any trouble—just come back tomorrow, OK?"

A big league Player.

A garbageman in charge of a monster truck. Lousy day. Cold. Rain. But he's a Player. This time the invitation comes from him. As I pass by, he says, "Hey, you look prosperous."

"Thank you. I feel prosperous."

"You look like a man who might have some frequent-flyer miles."

"As a matter of fact, I do. Lots of them."

"Listen, I need enough to get me to Buenos Aires, one way."

"I've got enough. They're yours. But what's in it for me?"

"Take the keys to this garbage truck. It's yours. Even trade."

Yes! I've long had an urge to drive one of those things. I'd like to dump a load of garbage in a certain person's front yard.

"It's a deal."

"You got a license to drive a truck?"

"Well, no."

"Deals off. I can't be part of anything illegal, but no problem. Get a license. I'm here every Monday."

As he drives off, I wonder how many other people on his route get offers from him every day.

He has all the nervy characteristics of a nonstop all-day Player.

It's early morning. Here's a lady standing at a bus stop. All seven people waiting with her have wires coming out of their ears. Radios, Ipods, Walkmans, or cell phones. All seven are in a zone—nodding heads in time to different music, staring off into space, or talking to invisible people.

Weird.

As I pass, I invite the lady to play: "They're all alien robots, you know. Their souls have been sucked out of them and exported." The lady gives me a hard look, moves closer to the curb, and stares down the street.

Not a Player.

A man who has just walked up says, "Yes, but they aren't useless. They're a street-theater company, and I'm their manager. We're on our way to a gig downtown."

"Really? What's the name of the performance?"

"Bus Stop Stupor. Look for us everywhere."

A Player.

———

One final example: A double whammy I didn't see coming.

Clerk in a bookstore—older lady with dyed red hair.

"Can I help you?" she asks.

"Happy birthday," I say. (Always makes people smile—sometimes you're early, sometimes late, but sometimes right on. An invitation to play.)

"Well, I hope you're coming to my party," she says. "We need someone to jump out of a cake."

"I'm your man."

"You'd be expected to go-go dance naked."

"Then I'm not your man."

"My mistake. I thought you looked a little kinky."

A Player.

A lady waiting in line behind me overheard this bookstore babble and drifted away from the counter and out the door. She missed her chance.

Probably not a Player.

Later, as I walked by a sidewalk table at a nearby coffeehouse, I spot the lady who fled the store. "Sorry, hope we didn't annoy you," I said.

She smiled. "Oh no," she replied, "It's just that I jumped out of the cake last year. It hurts my feelings to think they're looking for a replacement."

A Player after all.

29

Sidewalk News

"I am afraid of Vikings and parrots."

That sentence was written in white chalk on the sidewalk two blocks from my house. Several blocks away I found another message: *"I have three dead mittens."* And in the street many blocks further on, these words: *"My teeth sometimes leave my body at night."*

Well, then . . . So I bought some chalk . . .

Why not get into this person's game? Are they crazy or poetic or imaginative or looking for someone like them or just confused about the messages the world needs to be getting? Or maybe a Player? I don't know. Maybe it's a secret code between members of a non sequitur club or a message from an alien. Who cares? It would be interesting to know. Why miss the opportunity?

Ah, but what to write? Maybe some comments? This morning early I went back to the Unknown Chalker's statements, and wrote:

"The Vikings come bearing gifts."
"Parrots speak your mind."
"A fourth mitten has been found."
And *"Who needs faithful teeth?"*

And then I added at other locations, these inquiries:

"Will I ever learn?"
"Whatever became of me?"
"If you love me still, will you love me moving?"
"Who knew?"
"How do you plead?"
"Will the circle be unbroken?"

Granted, my words were not quite as obtuse as the Unknown Chalker's, but maybe I've raised the intellectual level of discourse.

Now it's a day later. Beginning to rain at daybreak. I rushed out to see if my challenge had been accepted. The rain had washed away most of the chalkings, but at two locations, in large block letters someone had printed:
"WHAT THE HELL IS GOING ON?"
Aha! There are three of us loose in the neighborhood with chalk. But I don't know if the last question is an addition to my questions or a cry of dismay. It is a good

question, you must admit. One most of us have muttered most of our lives—weekly, if not daily.

On the way home this afternoon I checked the sidewalk signboards, but the heavy rain had dissolved the chalk. It's just as well, I suppose. But I'm still thinking about how far this could go over time. And the next sunny day I'm going to write, *"WHY ME?"* That's the other great question we ask most of our lives.

The appearance of mysterious writing has been going on a long time. Things like this happened in the Bible, you know. Book of Daniel 5:24–28. *"Mene, Mene, Tekel, Parsin."* The words appeared on the wall during a feast given by Belshazzar, king of Babylon. Daniel interpreted the message to mean "You have been weighed in the balance and found wanting."

Bad news. Belshazzar may well have asked:

"What the hell is going on?" and "Why me?"

30

Taking Chances

Major event this past weekend: a sleepover at my house—with two beautiful young women and a handsome young man—all three with an intense interest in learning the rudiments of investment strategizing and financial risk taking.

Or, to put it less abstractly, two seven-year-old girls and a nine-year old boy—cousins—spent the night with their grandfather me learning poker. Five-card draw, to be specific.

Oh, they know about poker. They've seen it on TV. Their parents play, as do some of their older cousins and friends. But, like driving a car, poker is best not learned from a parent. By family consensus this is a job for grandfather. And these are the last three in the family who do not know the game. The time has come.

It was a little awkward to begin with. First of all, I kept my distance, having caught pinkeye from them the last time they stayed at my house. And they were grumpy right way about my rule that eating ice cream cones while playing cards was not OK. Also I was clearly out of my mind to think they would play with their own money. *"What? No way!"*

There were some small glitches to overcome: Getting them to say "Queens" instead of "Old Maids," convincing them that it doesn't matter that all the faces on the face cards are not looking in the same direction, and making them put all their cards back in the deck for another game when they wanted to hold on to their good cards for next round.

Bluffing was a stumbling block. When I explained that sometimes you must pretend you had good cards when you didn't, the grandson asked, "Isn't that lying?" Well, yes, in a way.

"I'm not good at lying," said a granddaughter, but then she admitted, "I like to lie and I lie all the time. It's just that I'm not good at it." Perfect. Every poker game needs an inept greenhorn.

A victim of the first hand dropped out. She didn't want to lose any more money. "But that's my money," said grandfather. "Not anymore," she explained.

Using all the extra loose poker chips, she started a make-believe cookie factory on the kitchen table. The

second loser soon joined her. So grandfather is left playing three hands against one grandson, and grandfather is
deliberately losing to keep him in the poker game and out
of the cookie operation in the kitchen.

"Stick to men's work," I advised him.

After a while it occurs to grandfather that grandson
knows exactly what is going on and is willing to go along
and take all of grandfather's money. Fortunately, the make-
believe cookies were ready and the girls needed a cus-
tomer, and since grandson had won all that money, maybe
he would buy some. And he did. Leaving grandfather alone
at the table, six dollars in the hole.

Why is it I think I know more about poker than they
do? Why is it I worry if the younger generation is as smart
as mine? Why is it I ended up buying all the rest of the
cookies *and* the cookie factory *and* cleaning up the cookie
mess as well? Why did I not notice that the cookie makers
had no qualms about making cookies out of ice cream
and poker chips?

This is how wisdom comes to grandfather: By being
taken to the cleaners by my own genetic spawn.

Finally, bedtime. Like most little kids, they like scary
stories.

"You can't scare us," they say.

"How much would you like to bet?"

"All the money we won at poker."

Oh, really? Well, then.

Lie down and hold on.

There's the story about the one-eyed old man who was always teased by little children. He hated little kids. They didn't know he could see through walls with his one eye. And they didn't know he grew pencil snakes, which are long and thin, with razor-sharp teeth. At night he would slip his snakes into a bedroom and the snakes would be drawn to the open eyes of little kids. In seconds the snakes would eat their way in through the open eyes and eat up the kid's brain and then eat its way out through the other eyeball, while the kid was screaming but couldn't be heard because the snake ate so fast he disconnected their voice. Horrible way to die.

"Is this true?"

"What do you think?"

(Silence.)

Three little children, eyes tightly closed, curled up in one bed together, didn't move. As I went to my room, I heard one small voice say, "Don't open your eyes."

I can't really say I'm six bucks ahead, because it was my money in the first place. But as I see it, we're even. I won my money back. They got their money's worth. And my seniority is intact: they know I still have a few cards up my sleeve. I may be old and stupid, but I'm still scary. I even manage to scare myself. I kept my eyes closed all night. It's a safe bet I wouldn't want to take any unnecessary chances with pencil snakes.

31

My Fault

It's been my fault all day today.
It's always my fault on Sundays.

Explanation: In my Seattle household there are seven of us: five core family, a housekeeper, and a large stuffed toy moose. We have instituted a scapegoat system of blame. Each person takes a turn and whatever around the house goes wrong or cockeyed, that person is at fault that day.

We're well organized. For example, the housekeeper is to blame on Saturdays, which is easy, because she's not even there. John, the stuffed moose, is to blame on Tuesdays. And Sunday is my day. Everybody else has his own special day as well.

The moose started it. A sad-eyed gray-plush creature, the size of a large dog, he has been around the house so long we forget how he got here—a gift from somebody for some reason. And my nineteen-year-old Japanese niece took pity on him, adopted him as a companion, and named him John.

One morning when I was raging around the kitchen over who drank the last of the milk again and didn't go to the store for more again, in walked Myra with the moose. "John did it," she said, "and he's so very sorry." The moose did look guilty. We laughed. John took his chastisement gracefully. Milk crisis forgotten.

For a while after that, everything got blamed on the moose, who always accepted his martyrdom with silent dignity.

Then Myra complained that John was being unfairly ostracized. His burden was getting too heavy to bear. She said he was depressed.

Then and there we decided to share the blame with John.

The scapegoat's job is to apologize and grovel a little while asking for forgiveness, which is easy when you know and everybody else knows that you are not really to blame for whatever happened. What started out as a silly joke became our family way—because, in reality, it really works out well. And it certainly seems to be appreciated by the John the moose.

So today it's all my fault.

I haven't been home all day. All I had to do was come

in the door and say, "I'm really so very, very sorry." In return I got laughter and shouts of "We forgive you." Which
made me curious, not defensive, about what I did—since
I really didn't know. And I can be truly repentant about
spilling nail polish on the rug and breaking another plate
and forgetting to get milk again.

Absurd, you say. Of course, I say.

But we laugh a lot while going through this daily drill
of condemnation and repentance. We lose track of guilt
and blame in the process of being ridiculous about the
minor shortcomings and idiosyncrasies of our household.
Small-minded finding of fault has become a high-spirited
family game.

Everybody knows they could do better, but nobody
feels bad getting reminded in a secondary loony way.

There are a lot worse ways to live together with other
people.

I know.

I've tried them.

32

Neighborly Solutions

Saw my next-door neighbor with her hands clasped to her face in small-scale grief, while standing at the stern of a garbage truck, which had just dumped its accumulated rear load up and over into the fetid innards of its maw. "Can I help?"

She blurted out her story. First she shoved a cork down into a fine bottle of wine she was going to serve to her in-laws. Then she destroyed her fancy corkscrew trying to get the cork out, meanwhile covering herself and her kitchen with bright crimson stains when the cork all-of-a-sudden plunged into the bottle, causing a major blow-back of the wine.

Then she went to the store and got two standard tear-the-cork-out-by-sheer-force cheap corkscrews and a new bottle of fine wine, along with some milk and other things while she was at it. She thought she'd emptied all the groceries out of the paper bag, which she wadded up and put in the garbage, which she put in the kitchen can, which she hauled out to the big can out on the curb.

Later she couldn't find the corkscrews when she was ready to open the wine. She remembered when she heard the garbage truck. And ran out.

I told her one of my father's oft-told jokes. A man was sitting in a two-hole outhouse with another man. After he did his business, he pulled up his pants, and said, "Damn, I had a five dollar bill in my hand and I dropped it through the hole."

Turning to the other man—a friend—he said, "Loan me a hundred bucks. I need it immediately." His friend took out his wallet and gave him a hundred dollar bill, which the man immediately threw down the hole. "What the hell did you do that for?" asked his friend. "Well," said the man, "I ain't going down there for no lousy five bucks."

My neighbor smiled.

"Throw your wedding ring into the back of the garbage truck," I advised, "and I guarantee you'll find the corkscrews. Some solutions require a bigger problem."

Giving me her *I-know-you're-an-idiot-but-you're-harmless* look, she retreated in silence up her driveway and into her house.

I would have loaned her a corkscrew, but she was obsessed with the corkscrews in the garbage truck and her own series of mistakes that got them there.

The real solution lay in giving up the problem.

As is so often the case.

I've also vexed the neighbor lady who lives on the other side of me.

And I'm sorry, but not very.

She can't figure out why the theft alarm in her old diesel Mercedes keeps going off. She doesn't know it, but it all has to do with her dog, a friendly but neurotic mutt who barks relentlessly every nine seconds when he's outside and lonely.

(And I do mean exactly nine—I timed him.)

It drives her next-door neighbor, me, crazy when I am trying to read my evening paper. But I like the lady, and there's really nothing to be done about the dog. I think the dog is just old and weird like me. He will probably die before I do. I just have to wait him out.

Yesterday I discovered by accident that if I slammed my back door hard it would set off the old Mercedes's theft alarm. And the lady would come out. And the dog would shut up. Well, then . . . door slamming. . . .

It works, but it's not a lasting solution. I know that. But it's an amusing diversion. I'll settle for that. And it seems to have affected the dog. It only barks every seventeen seconds now. What can't be entirely fixed can be warped into a different problem.

Maybe I could get the dog to jump into the garbage truck . . .

33

Amateur Joy

The winter of '03. I remember. The Rockettes came to town at Christmastide—a road show version of New York's Radio City Music Hall spectacular, featuring the long-legged lovelies who dance in unison, kick high, and strut around to big band music. The hot ticket for Christmas. "You just gotta go!"

Spectacular is the operative word. And even more extravaganza was available that winter—a Big samurai movie, and a Big sailing-ship-battle movie, and another Big round of the Lord of the Rings, and the Big college football games, and the Big TV superspecial phantas-magorias.

All spectacular. All big, Big, BIG!

But somehow, hyperstimulation was not what I wanted for Christmas.

Some low-key joy would do. Amateur joy.

I remembered a conversation I had with a Greek

friend in a small village on the island of Crete. I asked why the Greeks minimalize the celebration of Christmas but go all-out for Easter. He explained that December Twenty-fifth was just a birthday. Everybody has a birthday. Easter, on the other hand, celebrates a resurrection from the dead. That's amazing. That's spectacular. That's Big.

Besides, by the end of December the Cretans have survived the stress of the tourist season, the exhaustion of the olive and orange harvest, and the first storms of the winter. Nobody is up for roasting lambs outdoors in the windy rain and dancing around in circles in the village square. A quiet church service, a walk home in the silent night, soup and bread, some old songs with family around a fire, and bed—that's it.

The work of amateurs.

And that would explain why on a Saturday night in December when I could have seen the Rockettes or gone to the symphony or watched explosions on a Big screen, I was somewhere else:

In a small Lutheran church in my neighborhood, listening to a choir of dedicated amateurs sing their hearts out. At the intermission there were home-baked cookies provided by the ladies of the church. And I bought a raffle ticket on a handmade Christmas quilt. The proceeds would be given to the needy in the neighborhood.

Then we returned to the sanctuary to hear a reading of Dylan Thomas' account of "A Child's Christmas in

Wales." Finally, the audience joined the choir in singing carols, ending with "Silent Night." Off-key, but sincere.

Unspectacular. No glitz, no glamor, no extravagance. No Big deal.

Walking home in the rain, I realized this was not a Lutheran deal or even a Christian one. It was about the universal Companionship of Amateurs of any faith or culture, struggling like me to feel at home in the winter's dark, and awed to be part of the Mystery of It All.

I wasn't excited when I went to bed. Just contented with getting what I wanted most so early in the holiday season: the company of people like me who find in themselves in the middle of winter a capacity for joy—small and deep and ordinary.

Amateur joy.

34

Intersection II

Moab, Utah, is a small town in the far four-corners area of the American Southwest—where the states of Arizona, New Mexico, Colorado, and Utah touch. The town is a green oasis in a land of red rock canyons, high desert plateaus, wild rapid rivers, snow capped mountains, and vast empty spaces. Most of the land is public—state and national forest and parks. Water is scarce. It's hot and windy in summer, cold and windy in winter, and arid in any season. Not many people—mostly Navajo Indians, Hispanics, Mormons, cowboys, dry-land bean farmers, ranchers, miners, and fossil hunters. Or that's the way it was.

Then the great outdoor recreation boom hit in the early Seventies. Hikers, river-runners, bicyclists, climbers, backpackers, jeepers, hunters, and just plain tourists discovered the area. They came to have a look and be in the middle of nowhere. And maybe stay awhile.

I was one of those—thirty years ago.

In spring and summer the town and the backcountry gets crowded.

But in autumn, when the aspens turn yellow and the first snows fall in the mountains, most of the recreational itinerants leave. And in winter it's quiet again. The town still has only five thousand year-around people. Many of the stores and restaurants and motels close. If you pass through Moab in winter at three o'clock in the morning on the way to somewhere, you might think the town has been abandoned.

For many years I have returned to this landscape in the quiet seasons. To a small house and art studio in a mountain valley twenty miles south of town. I go to get away from city life, to be in touch with myself, to shut my mouth and open my spirit, and to allow my senses to function free of the noise of civilization.

At least once a week I go into town for supplies. And I'm always surprised by what I find. Civilization seeps in somehow. There was a time when Moab was a cultural black hole. Now people and customs from across the world often appear, even in quiet seasons, and when I come home from town I usually bring back more than groceries and hardware . . .

35

Half a Conversation

If you were one of my distant neighbors from up the valley, and you dropped by for coffee-and-catch-up, and you asked me the "What's New?" question, I'd say I was in town yesterday, and you'd say, "And so . . ." and I'd share these experiences with you. Local news.

In The City Market, a voice over the public address system announced "We have fresh sushi in the meat department." *Sushi?* Oh sure. Probably frozen—not even Japanese—direct from Shanghai, China. Wrong. Miss Lucy Begay, a young Navajo Indian woman, was there turning out salmon rolls from scratch—much to the amused dismay of three Japanese visitors. Miss Lucy learned to make sushi from a Mexican guy in Albuquerque.

———

Farther up the aisle, I found that artesian water was on special—bottled in the Fiji Islands a thousand miles out in the middle of the Pacific Ocean and hauled all the way to Moab. Of course I bought some. This coffee is made with water from Fiji. Why not? And there's a bonus: Hold the empty bottle up to your ear, and you can hear the ocean and the sound of the surf out on the reef.

On my way into town I passed a long line of bikers riding in a fifty-mile bike tour for charity. On their way up and over the La Sal Mountains. The Halloween Lycra Brigade. Tight bodies, tight outfits, and nobody's wearing much underwear. Sexy. Even the former inhabitants—the Indians—couldn't have matched the ceremonial biker costumes.

At the first pit stop, the bikers were being urged on by the throbbing sound of the Moab Ladies' Taiko Drummers, pounding sound out of big Japanese drums. (Fueled, no doubt by fresh *sushi* from City Market.)

On the way back from town I stopped in at the annual Gem and Mineral Show held at the rodeo arena. Cultural subgroups fascinate me. All these people whose lives revolve around fossils and rocks, for example. One guy was selling what he swore was reptile coprolite—fossilized turtle feces 150 million years old. Yes. How does he know? But I didn't have any so I took his word for it and bought a piece. Look. And now you can say you know a guy who has some. And the next time I go in for my annual physical exam, I'll take it along as a stool sample.

A young man at the show was demonstrating flint knapping—the art of making arrow and spear points out of flint and obsidian. He's way beyond doing what the local Indians did. His expertise includes making museum-quality Clovis and Folsum points of superb quality. Even more, he was selling a video of his shaping Danish weapons from stone. A dagger was on display. The Vikings probably used these as a sidearm.

Genealogists say my family originated in eighth-century Denmark, so I was drawn to the dagger. It must have vibrated something in my DNA because I left thinking about going pillaging this afternoon. If I only had a bronze helmet . . .

I noticed in the paper that next week in the same rodeo arena women on horses will be racing in a clover-leaf pattern around fifty-five-gallon drums—barrel racing. And the cross-country unicyclists will be in town. And a convention of jugglers. And a traveling tattoo-and-piercing show. And on Saturday night, a performance in Star Hall of a bluegrass band all the way from the Czech Republic.

Who knows what's next?

That would be my report to my neighbor—the answer to "What's new?" As I say, I used to come here to far Southeast Utah because not much was going on and the world seemed so far away.

Now, well, this is the world. As it is.

Not so very far away at all.

As amazing as it always was, I suppose, if one stays alert.

And late last night, after the sky cleared following a lightning-thunder-and-rain storm, I heard the sounds of the tail end of a party at the ranch in the valley below my house. A voice cried out, "Oh, God, Where Are You, God?" and an echoing voice replied, "Coming, dear."

How about you? What's new?

36

Cowboys

Four generations of the men in my family were horsemen.

As we say in Texas, where I grew up, I have "cowboy" in my genes/jeans. In my youth I worked on ranches and rode in rodeos for seven summers. My cowboy gear is in a trunk in the basement: big black hat, worn jeans, leather chaps, beat-up boots, rusty spurs, well-used saddle, and even bull-riding gear. Now and then I still get cowboyed-up and ride around on a horse.

Sentimental pleasure. But nobody's fooled. I'm not for real.

I saw a real working cowboy recently on my way into town. He was pushing a small herd of pudgy cows from winter pens onto leased grazing land. The angle of the sun said spring is not far off, but the barbed-wire wind insisted winter's not finished. So the cowboy was hunkered down deep in the saddle on his mud-spattered brown mare.

The hood of a dirty gray-down parka covered his head. Underneath the hood he wore a red-plaid wool baseball cap with earflaps tied under his chin. Under the parka I could see a ratty army-surplus wool sweater over faded brown-duck insulated overalls. No chaps. No spurs, either, because they wouldn't fit on his insulated rubber tundra boots, all slimed up with manure and mud.

Scratched sunglasses hung on his sunburned nose and brown stains dribbled down his stubbled chin—the overflow juice from the cigarette butt he's just chewing on because it's too windy to smoke.

John Wayne he's not. He looks more like a war refugee than a cowboy. If they used him as a model in a cigarette advertisement, more people would give up smoking.

I stopped to talk.

"Where're you headed with this sorry bunch of mud-balls?"

"I've a mind to drive 'em all the way to Miami Beach."

"Won't that take a long time?"

"Sure, but what's time to a cow?"

We laugh. But not much. It's an old joke.

"I thought you were happy cowboying right here in San Juan County."

"Are you crazy? Cowboying gets meaner every year. Price of beef is going down and the price of feed is way up. And mad-cow disease—that's a laugh! You don't get it if you eat 'em, you get it if you try to make a living off 'em.

"Worse, if you raise or sell or even, God forbid, eat beef

these days you're looked upon as the devil by all them activists. Somebody put an 'EAT BEEF AND DIE' bumper sticker on my pickup truck. I covered it up with another sticker that says, 'SAVE A COW, EAT A VEGETARIAN.'"

"No more glamour and romance?"

"Nah, cowboying's gone to hell. It's nasty, hard, poor-paying work. You got to be an idiot to want to do this for a living."

"Why do you keep doing it?"

"I'm an idiot!" he shouted, as he rode off after his cows.

Still, he is the real thing—a real cowboy. But not for long, I think. I saw him a few days later in a local café. Says he'd like something else to ride. Something that won't buck—something he won't have to feed. He wants a motorcycle. A Harley. And he'd like to look like one of those black-leather, bad-ass biker dudes, wheeling free down the highway in the wind. To hell with cowboying!

The only people I know who are still serious about horses are the weekend indoor-arena buckaroos. Their game is calf roping and two-man steer roping. It's a wanna-be sport. Most of these guys are construction contractors, ostrich farmers, car dealers, plumbers, and bankers with town jobs who want to be cowboys. They wear baseball caps and low-heel, round-toed, lace-up athletic boots made for walking and running. And they bathe every day. Cowboy? Home on the range? Fat chance.

Sometimes in town I see men dressed like they think real cowboys dress. Handlebar moustache, clean-shaven, sweet-smelling. Wearing high-heeled, pointy-toed, snake-skin boots, pressed jeans, horse-hair belt with a buckle the size of a coffee-cup saucer, a green-and-black-striped silk Western shirt with pearl snaps, a fringed-and-beaded buckskin jacket, and a great big white cowboy hat. Cowboys? No. Probably interstate truck drivers or German tourists.

When I see a swarthy man with black hair wearing a black felt cowboy hat, white Western shirt, Wrangler jeans, belt with a turquoise-and-silver buckle, and black cowboy boots, I know he's not a cowboy, either. He's an Indian. Native American. Navajo. The conservative cowboy look is now standard dress code for Indians. Go figure.

A semi-final fashion note. All the cowboy and Indian kids dress alike. Basketball shoes, baggy pants, oversize athletic shirts, and baseball cap on backward. They don't want to be cowboys or Indians. They want to be Black Homeboys. Maybe this is social progress—a sign of integration.

The ultimate fashion step away from real cowboying can be seen in the clothes in the fancy Western boutiques in Moab. I tried on a black-and-white leather jacket, fitted with silver conchos, bone beads, and about five feet of leather fringe. On the back were stitched the words: BAD BANDITOS. It's the ultimate in macho—a combination of cowboy, Indian, and motorcycle gang. Locals call this garb "rooster suits"—clothes to strut around in. A truly manly piece of apparel. (That's good.) And I could wear it out of the store for only one thousand dollars. (That's bad.) Of course I tried it on. I'm a guy. Cock-a-doodle-do. But strutting is not my style.

I bet my cowboy friend will want one of these outfits when he gets the Harley Davidson motorcycle he's saving up for. The screwball truth—the final fashion irony—is that the only real cowboy I know yearns to ride a hog, not a horse, and dress like a Hollywood-Indian-Biker-Dude.

All this is harmless enough, I suppose. Life is a costume party. And if part of who we really are is who we'd like to pretend to be, then we might as well have the right outfit for it.

37

About Water—Poem Left on the Pillow of a Houseguest Who Seemed Lost and Confused

Are you are reading these words
Because you've been looking
For something?
Something to hold onto?
A talisman for this day?
Reading this, like walking
Up a dry streambed in September?
Looking for something for your pocket;
A keepsake for taking home;
Kindling to start the fire of memory;
Looking for whatever the flash floods
Of August have picked up, polished,
Washed down and offer you now:
Smooth stones, sanded sticks,
Feathers, bones, seeds,
And unspeakable sounds

That break the logjam of being.
Are you are walking up the dry bed
Of this poem looking
For something like that?
To have, to hold, to keep?

Stop.
Go back.
Wait until the big storm comes in you.
Be here when the flood flashes through.
Stand in the water as deep as you dare.
If what the water does is lost on you,
Then you are truly lost.
Wait.
Stay until you know
What water does.
Hold onto that.
Finder's keeper's.

38

The Train to Birmingham

Place: Sunday morning at the Moab Diner, where the clock on the wall runs backward, the waitresses call you "Hon," and the eggs, bacon, potatoes, and toast are all served up dry and crisp and fast.

Four men sat down in the booth next to mine. Big men in camouflage hunting fatigues. They looked so much alike I asked if they were related. Yes. Four generations, actually— son age seventeen, father thirty-eight, grandfather fifty-eight, and the great-grandfather, eighty. A rowdy, outgoing quartet.

Over breakfast they told tall tales and jokes and laughed a lot.

Going elk hunting, they said. Not to kill anything. Just to spend one more week in camp in the mountains. To see the aspens turn yellow, to walk in the first snow of the season, to hear the elks bugle, and to sit by a fire as night falls. But mostly just to be together.

Lucky men. I envied them.

My thoughts turned to a man named John Howard. He lived in Muscle Shoals, Alabama, a small town in the northwest corner of the state, on the banks of the upper Tennessee River. He came there in the late nineteenth century after the American Civil War. It was said that he was descended from the English Howard family. The title of Duke of Norfolk, the oldest dukedom in England, passed to a John Howard in 1483. The Howards retain the title to this day. Anne Boleyn, mother of Elizabeth I, and Catherine Howard were both members of the family— and both were beheaded by their loving but frustrated husband, Henry VIII.

John Howard of Muscle Shoals, Alabama, was an un-royal druggist, married, with two sons and three daughters. He must have been unhappy with his life. One morning the burden finally became unbearable.

He dressed for work as usual, stopped by his drugstore to empty the safe of cash, and went out the door headed for the train station. The assistant druggist went with him. A young woman. Witnesses said neither Mr. Howard nor his companion carried a suitcase. It must have been a spur-of-the-moment decision. He actually did what a lot of us think of doing in a hopelessly miserable situation: Just get up and go—now—disappear.

This John Howard was my maternal grandfather. Until I was well into adulthood I thought he was dead. That's what I was led to believe. But I also thought it odd that he was never ever mentioned by my mother, grandmother, or aunts and uncles or cousins.

No memories.

No photographs.

Finally, an aunt, her tongue loosened by one too many bourbons, blurted out the truth. Or at least the minimal story. "He caught the morning train for Birmingham . . . and the son-of-a-bitch never came back."

What became of him? Nobody knows.

What was his side of the story? Nobody knows.

I wonder what he thought about on the train to Birmingham.

Maybe he considered running away to be a better solution to an unhappy marriage than Henry VIII's homicidal choice. I wonder if he thought about what he would miss by running away. I wonder if he ever imagined the possibility of somebody like me. A grandson. Sitting in a booth in the Moab Diner one fall Sunday morning wishing he had a grandfather.

The men in the booth next to me joked with the waitress as they left. Their tip for her was generous. I watched them pile into their big truck and head off down the highway. Oh how I wanted to go with them.

I thought about John Howard of Muscle Shoals, Alabama.

If he had missed that train, he might be here this morning. And I would take him with me to the mountains, a long way from Birmingham.

39

Meditation on the
Death of a Fly

The first warm day of onrushing spring rallied the dormant bug population of my house. As school locker rooms spill teams of amateur athletes onto practice fields at this season, the egg sacs in the darkest corners of my study burst forth legions of tiny spiders onto the floor and launch waves of minute flying midges onto the wall. No cause for exterminating action for me. Experience has taught me patience. Within hours the baby bugs will be lunch for a small team of freshman lizards.

On a slightly larger scale, the Dispersal Committee of the Housefly Commune has already assigned one juvenile fly to each room of my house. These newly licensed pilots move with maniacal speed, zooming erratically here and there, practicing upside-down landings on the ceilings, crashing into the clear window glass, and corkscrewing through the air in acrobatic shows of skill—but seldom landing long enough for me to get a shot at them with my Great Yellow Swatter of Death.

There are also a few tenacious survivors left over from the end of winter. For two days now a fat, elderly fly has lived out his last hours on the top of my desk. His airborne adventures seem to have ended. Slowly he walks from one end of the desk to another, pausing at the edge, and walking back again to the other end and another edge. He does not bother me. I do not bother him. It is in his favor that he has lost the urge, the will, or the ability to launch himself into the air. As long as he does not enter my No Fly Zone, I am content.

Once he even heaved himself up onto the Great Yellow Swatter of Death, walked its length, tumbled off the end and walked on. Fearless. Dignified. Senile.

This morning he is still present, though moving ever so slowly, a centimeter or two at a time. At this moment he rests between me and the computer screen, scratching and patting his head with his two front feet. Perhaps he is reflecting on the distance to the far away edge of the table. He sighs and plods on.

I worry about him.

What is there for an old fly to eat or drink on the hard brown desert of my desk? Will he fall off the edge the next time he gets there and break his neck? Or try his wings one last desperate time before he nosedives into the tile floor? Do his children know where he is, or care?

Can he see me, the possible agent of his fate, and is he afraid? Does he anticipate the coming of the Great Lizard, or is he comforted by knowing that, like mutton, he is too tough and stringy to be eaten now?

I can't ignore him—there he is, creeping back and forth.

I can't push him off the table—too cruel.

And I can't quite bring myself to smash him dead—too easy.

So I put a jar over him and peered at him through a magnifying glass. Unlike other insects I've investigated, he did not panic—no mad rushing about or trying to escape. He looks tired and gray. Slowly he wrings his hands. When I removed the jar, he resumed walking toward the edge again with great dignity and purpose. Just before I turned off the light to go to bed, he was walking in circles, slowly, slowly, slowly . . .

This morning I found him lying on his back. Dead.

With respect for his dignity and mine, I took him outside for burial. With a teaspoon I dug a small grave for him beneath a weed that is just coming into bright red bloom.

A unique event, however trivial. The first fly funeral I had attended. I pondered the sense of mercy that stayed my hand from the Great Yellow Swatter of Death. What kept me from automatically smashing the life out of the vulnerable senior fly? Soft-hearted folly or seasoned wisdom?

Being culturally wired to detest flies and kill them at any opportunity, what got into me? Briefly we were the only two living things in the room. Struggling on as long as possible. The spark of life in him and the spark of life in me was the same. We were connected. Live and let live.

Now I understand what it means when people say:

"He wouldn't hurt a fly."

That can happen.

40

Night Thoughts

Cosmic notions rose up out of the swamplands of my mind last night. I sat outside on the porch at 3:00 a.m. wrapped in an old green bathrobe, focusing on the Milky Way with my binoculars.

(If you are impressed that I should be stargazing at that hour of the night, don't be. The goddammed packrats—more later on them—were having a potluck party in my bedroom wall, and as long as I was wide awake, I might as well use the opportunity to check the sky.)

I am in a "Zone of Darkness." Make of the statement what you will, but the term refers to a location favorable for the requirements of astronomy. Southeastern Utah is one of the few areas of the United States where light-scatter from centers of civilization is minimal—making viewable light from cosmic sources maximal.

Simply said, you can see the stars from here.

Lots and lots and lots of stars. Even more than that.

So my subscriptions to astronomy magazines come to Moab, and I read them to be astonished. And, monthly, I am. For example, "Spiral galaxy NGC 300 in 'Sculptor' is larger than previously believed—by a factor of two or greater." The increasing power of our telescopes means we can now see what we missed before: There are so many stars in that galaxy that it's actually twice as big as we thought—maybe even larger.

"And so what?" you ask.

Here's the kicker: The article goes on to explain that "Our galaxy is much more massive and brighter than NGC 300, so ours is probably twice as large as we previously thought—perhaps as much as 200,000 light years across."

Concentrate on the idea.

Our galaxy. Twice as large as we thought.

The news didn't even make the daily papers.

But I sense the implications of this information when I look up at the Milky Way and see a gazillion stars in a great sky river, and then look through binoculars and see a bazillion stars I couldn't see before. All we lacked to be able to know the size of our galaxy was more sensitive equipment. And when our equipment improves again—which is likely—we will no doubt be even more astonished by what we can see and know.

The Theory of Intelligent Design says that creation is so immense and so complex that a point is reached where its very incomprehensibility is evidence that a Being beyond us must have designed it. Which is like saying that since barnacles on the side of a cruise ship can't possibly ever comprehend the complexities or purpose of the great passenger liner they're riding on, there must be a God of the Barnacles who made it. And put it there just for the barnacles. And takes care of it for their benefit.

No. I don't think so.

When I read that Einstein failed to figure out a Unified Theory of Everything and died thinking that the universe was ultimately incomprehensible, I realized I could scratch the problem off my own list. And I went back to focusing on the few things I did comprehend.

Not knowing everything doesn't mean not knowing some things.

"Agnostic" is not a bad word.

A limitation of tools and intelligence is not proof of anything except a limitation of tools and intelligence. The barnacles will never comprehend the cruise ship. They cannot. The barnacles, like us, are pretty much on their own. Meanwhile, like us, they are plunging on, holding on tight, sometimes enduring and sometimes enjoying the amazing ride.

As I have for the last hour.

41

Bling!

There is a *Neotoma cinerea* on the porch of my house.

In a little wire cage—a humane trap.

The creature is about the size of a squirrel, plain dusty brown, with dark chocolate eyes and a long, furry tail. He or she? How can I tell?

If I could hold the cage up for your inspection, you might join the chorus of two visiting neighbor ladies, whose spontaneous response was:

"Oooh . . . It's so cute. Poor little thing. What is it?"

Want to see it? Wait. First I'll tell you the critter's common names:

Rat. Western Bushy-Tailed Pack Rat.

"Oh, well, then . . ."

Rat is a pejorative word. Rat = Bad.

Hereinafter I'll refer to my temporary captive as "Mrs. Packer."

One of her relatives worked its way into my house this winter while I was away. The caretaker set the humane trap and caught it. But not before it had eaten part of a cowhide rug and the soft parts of a pair of deerskin moccasins and the tongues of my hiking boots. And it made a nest inside the living-room wall, packing it with cactus parts, rabbit brush, and half a roll of shredded paper towels.

After I arrived in early spring, the gnawing sounds in the wall in the middle of the deep velvet silence of the night told me what I did not want to know: there's never just one Packer in a nest. And, quoting the *Field Guide to Western Mammals,* "Probably 1 or 2 litters per year of 2 to 6."

The Packers are nervous now that I'm here. The guide explains: "When alarmed, they will engage in hind-foot-drumming or produce a slow tapping sound." That explains the midnight jazz concert:

Diddy-drum-diddy-drum-gnaw-gnaw-diddy diddy drum . . .

Worse. The guide goes on to say that a nest can be used by generations of the Packer Family—for hundreds of years—providing ecologists with clues to environmental changes. That's because of the Packer's peculiar habit of collecting: "cow dung, bones, rocks, sticks, cans, and especially any shiny objects to decorate the nest." They protect their collection with pads of spiny prickly pear—the Packer Family security system. Wouldn't want some bandit critter to burgle the family jewels.

Interesting. But trouble, just the same. Sure, I'm going to trap them all, and deport them, but in the meantime, how about this "shiny objects" business?

Curious, I collected odds and ends of shiny stuff and scattered it around the porch: chewing gum wrappers, a dime and a quarter, two or three small shards of a broken mirror, some wads of aluminum foil, a couple of metal screws, a steel ball bearing, and a beer can pull tab.

The first to be snatched up was the chewing gum wrapper. Wrigley's Juicy Fruit. I imagine the conversation in the nest when Mr. Packer showed up with the treasure. "Oh, no, not another damned gum wrapper!" said his spouse. "We've got way too many gum wrappers. The nest smells like fruit salad."

"Well, dear, there's a bonanza out there."

"Great! Go get some more shiny stuff."

"How about a piece of mirror?"

"Yes!"

After the mirror, the next to disappear were the metal screws, the steel ball-bearing and the beer can pull-tab. And in two night's work, all the shiny stuff was hauled away. Now it's all inside my wall.

Shiny stuff. What on earth does shiny stuff have to do with the survival of the Packer species? What kink in the genetic make-up drives these little furry creatures to collect and decorate their nest with shiny stuff?

Can't eat it. Can't wear it. Can't sell it.

Can't live without it.

Long after this packrat encounter, I met a wildlife biologist on a plane and told my story. She explained: "They really do it. We call it 'nuptial gifting'—because it's meant to attract the opposite sex."

"No! Nuptial gifting? Get serious."

"Oh, yes. It's true. And apparently it works."

When I went to town today to fetch more humane traps, I had an epiphany. Everywhere I looked I saw shiny stuff. Rings, watches, necklaces, earrings, belly-button hardware, belt buckles, hair clips, and pins. Silver, gold, platinum, diamonds, and rhinestones.

And chrome—lots of chrome—on cars and motorcycles and dump trucks and bicycles and scooters and jeeps and dune-buggies and eighteen-wheel freight liners. Guystyle shiny stuff.

The hip-hop generation calls shiny stuff "Bling-bling." And the more glitz you wear on your body, the better. The more excited you will make members of the opposite sex. And since you can't wear it all at any one time, you keep drawers of it at home. Mondo maximum Bling!

Can't eat it. Can't live without it.

As I write this, I stop and consider the *Neotoma cinerea* in the cage out on the porch. She's quiet and still. Being a nocturnal creature by nature, I suppose she's sleepy, having been up all night and now all day. She doesn't know she's on the cusp of fame because when I finish this her story gets flung out into the world. She's probably thinking that . . . if she'd just foregone her gum wrapper mania . . . done without the mirror . . . she'd be home in bed by now.

But she has to go. We can't go on living together like this. Her drumming and gnawing in the middle of the night drives me crazy. And my pounding on the walls and shouting doesn't faze her or her jazz combo.

Having surveyed my own collection of shiny stuff, I do feel a sympathetic kinship with the Packers. When my own midden is dug up by some anthropologist a thousand years from now, he will wonder, as I do now, "What the hell use was all this shiny stuff?"

Having selected a new neighborhood for her up the creek, I will carefully release Mrs. Packer this afternoon. And if I catch any more of her family, I'll take them to the same place. And leave some starter shiny stuff around to make them feel at home as a gesture of empathetic good-will.

"Ooooh look! Gum wrappers!"

Bling!

42

Guest Towel

Sunrise. Good morning!
Here, this dark green towel is for you.
Far away and long ago are its threads.
Woven from long-staple Egyptian cotton of the Nile delta,
Dyed in the vats of Istanbul.
Shipped across wide seas and plains to this place.
Washed in water from an aquifer a thousand feet deep,
ten million years old.
Hung out in yesterday afternoon's sunlight
In the clear high desert air at seven thousand feet.
Soaking up indigo from the sky.
Verdigris is the name of its color.

All through the night the towel remained outside.
Stardust from the Milky Way fell on it.
When the thunderstorm rolled through this
valley at three in the morning,

Lightning recharged the towel's batteries.
Raindrops blown from the Gulf of Mexico soaked
into the towel.
The night wind dried the towel.
The morning sun ironed the towel flat.
The towel is ready.

Take it—it's just for you.
Stand outside in the chilly morning under the outdoor shower.
(Be careful—there's frost on the deck boards.)
Wash yourself under the steamy water.
And when you are wet and warm and clean,
Reach for this towel, and hold it to your face.
Breathe deep. Smell it.
Dry yourself slowly, slowly.
Wrap the towel around you and stand before the mirror.
Look.
You are clothed in a royal garment.
The time being is all you have,
And for the time being, the news of your realm is good.

43

Charley-Up-a-Tree

A Moab "true story"—part fact, part gossip, part imagination.

Charley has been up in a tree in his own yard for almost a week.

Big old cottonwood with a four-limb pocket at the first branching.

The place in a tree any kid would say is perfect for a tree house.

Charley's up there with a sleeping bag and basic supplies.

He's attached himself to a limb with a rope and some bungee cords.

He doesn't want to fall out.

And he's not coming down on his own. Ever.

———

Shirley, his wife, found him up there Friday night.

She stood under the tree staring at him, and he stared back.

She knew why he was up there, so there was no use asking.

She thought that *bygod* he got up there, he could *bygod* get down.

Then the neighbors noticed.

But he wouldn't talk to them.

He knew they knew—and shared Shirley's position.

"Get down on your *bygod* own, you silly bastard."

Even Charley's friend Willy couldn't get him to come down.

But Willy did take a rain tarp and some more food up to him.

There was talk of involving a minister or a psychiatrist.

But everybody knows what Charley thinks of "people-shrinkers."

Three days later someone finally called 911.

And the fire department came—they had been expecting the call.

Charley wouldn't talk to them or use the ladder they put up.

It's a small town. Volunteer fire department.

They already knew he was up there. And why.

Some of the firemen secretly admired him.

Two of them considered joining him.

Married guys with issues of their own.

There's no law against his being up in his own tree.

Though people are starting to drive by and stare and honk.

And some kids threw dirt clods at him, but he's too high up to hit.

Eddie the cop told him he could be cited as a public nuisance.

But Pam from the tourist office said he could be a local attraction.

Maybe they could charge for photo opportunities.

Nobody really understands.

He's not coming down.

Ever.

Charley read a book about that young woman tree-hugger.

She stayed up in a redwood tree for two years.

She finally got her way, too. Saved the tree.

As for Charley, he's not so sure of the outcome of his exile.

His old cottonwood isn't worth saving.

But something will happen. Sooner or later.

———————

Of course, all of this—all of it—is a daydream, so far.

Charley's in his Lazy-Boy armchair staring at the weather on TV.

He can imagine his move to the tree.

He's talked about doing it around town so long that both he and a few others think that maybe he actually did it.

But he hasn't really done it.

Because the reason is so damn dumb.

He'd have to leave town if people knew.

See, it's about the eggs.

For thirty years he's eaten the eggs Shirley cooks.

He wants over-easy-and-runny; she cooks sunny-side-up-and-hard.

They don't talk about it anymore.

He hates the way Shirley cooks his eggs.

He knows. She knows. What's to say?

But it drives him mad.

So he eats his eggs and plans his move.

And considers how things might play out—the consequences.

In truth, it's not just the eggs.

Their whole life has become one big stalemate.

If he just up and left, she'd win.

Killing her is illegal, and the eggs aren't cooked any better in jail.

Killing himself is painful and messy.

Cannibalism is possible, but she'd probably taste as bad as her eggs.

And he's *bygod* not going to cook his own eggs.

That's women's work.

In thirty years the only solution he's come up with is tree exile.

And Monday afternoon, *bygod,* he's going to do it.

If it doesn't rain.

44

A New Year, New Broom

Many people are missing from Moab this week. The ones who went off to visit relatives. The ones who went away to the mountains to ski. And those who went to Mexico or Hawaii or Florida to bask on a beach. Me, I like being around when the town is deserted and quiet. Traveling during the holidays is a nightmare. I am where I want to be. So I have stayed put.

When I have come across my fellow Stay-Putters in town, I've asked what they've been up to in this calm between holidays. Like me, they observe the Season of Small Rituals. The marking of a new cycle in a low-key way.

Here's my accumulated list of what they did:

Turned the mattresses on the beds.
Defrosted the refrigerator.
Paid year-end bills and balanced a checkbook.

Cleaned out and reorganized a drawer, a closet, a
     basement, a garage.
Bought new tires for a car and had it serviced.
Bought new bathroom soap and shampoo.
Made kids clean up their rooms—as well as can be
     expected.
Had a manicure, pedicure, haircut, or hairdo.
Cleaned out the medicine cabinet in the bathroom.
Bought new sponges and dishtowels for the kitchen.
Revised an address book based on Christmas card
     receipts.
Made two trips to the Good Will with Stuff.
Washed out and sanitized all the plastic wastebaskets.

Me, I bought a new broom. The old-fashioned kind.
Handmade, heavy-duty one. Plain wood handle, sweet-
smelling pale yellow straw with black stitching. The old
one was worn down and deformed from being much used
and left standing too long in a corner. And, on close examination, it looked and smelled rancid from all the grubby
uses it had been put to in the year past.

What to do with an old broom? The truth? Last night I
dipped the straw in kerosene, lit it, and threw the broom
from the front porch in a high arc, like a burning spear or
falling star. WooHa! It landed in the snow. Why did I do
this, you ask? Just for the hell of it, I suppose. I'd never
done it before, so why not? Somehow putting it in the
garbage seemed a waste of an opportunity. (*If you do this,*

it's a good idea to have snow around. And don't aim for trees.)

The new broom is fecund with opportunities, especially if you are alone. It can be used to play air guitar with rock and roll on the radio. Or as an air bass with bluegrass music. A new broom makes a good dancing partner—nobody gets hurt when you do deep dips or swing it over your shoulder.

Of course, there are other uses for a broom. It's a versatile tool. A weapon against weird bugs, spiders, and mice. Excellent cobweb remover. Good for poking things out from under places you can't or don't want to put your hands—under beds or from behind the washer. I've often used mine for coaxing small birds down from the rafters when they've flown inside the house by mistake. Brooms are superb for doing balancing tricks to impress small children. (I can do it on my chin.) And now, of course, I can look forward to the flaming spear event at year's end when the broom wears out.

On reflection, I see this new broom as my symbol of an existential need to clean house mentally and spiritually at this time of the year. To sweep away small sorrows, to throw out small grievances, to clear off the clutter of irrelevant things-to-do lists from the workshop of my life.

All too soon the new broom will become the old broom from use. The fuss and mess and bother of my life will accumulate again. It's a cycle. Maybe that's the deeper reason I took such pleasure in lighting the old broom and throwing it in the evening darkness out into the snow, marking the cycle, punctuating the possibilities of a new year with primitive fireworks. WooHa!

(Tell a friend and word gets around and strange things happen. In the first week of the New Year the local Moab newspaper printed a picture of a group of people setting their brooms on fires in the parking lot of the local radio station on New Year's Eve. Friends of mine. The caption said the broom burners claimed it was " an ancient medieval European tradition.")

45

Intersection III

Each year for more than twenty years I have spent several months on the Greek island of Crete. Why Crete? I might say it's because I like history. More than six thousand years of human events are piled up there. I could say it's the beauty of the landscape—mountains, sea, and beaches. But the main incentive to return again and again is the people—the Cretans. I have binding connections with them, their view of life, and their way with strangers.

What are Cretans like? Like this . . .

46

Asbestos Gelos

My Cretan connection began the summer I was wandering around Europe alone while waiting for my wife to finish her medical residency. No particular agenda—just doing what came next. I went to Crete to see the famous archaeological digs at Knossos and to look in on a graduate school program at the Orthodox Academy of Crete. When I was ready to step off the paths beaten down by tourists, I went to a small village at the western end of the island—a fishing village at the end of the road: Kolymbari.

I found a room for the night and rose before the sun the next morning to go running. The day was already hot, so I dressed only in black running briefs and shoes. (It's relevant to the story to note here that my hair and beard were white even then.) My route took me past the main *kofeneion* (coffeehouse) of the village where men sat outside socializing. They ignored me. I was surprised. They seemed surly, hostile, and unwelcoming.

Later, when I mentioned this to my landlord, he said, "Oh no, Cretans are very welcoming to strangers—it is an old tradition—*philoxenia*. But in your case the men at the *kofeneion* did not know what to make of you. For one thing, your hair and beard make you look like a priest, but they have never seen a half-naked priest running through the village in what looks like his underwear at that hour of the morning."

"Oh."

"No problem. Smile, wave, say good morning in Greek: *Kalimera*—kah-lee-mare-ah. You will find them friendly."

"Right."

(Pause.)

See this from the point of view of the men at the *kofeneion*. They have been gathering here at dawn for years without disturbance or distraction. Suddenly, without warning, the white-bearded, half-naked priest flashes by.

"What the hell was that, Yorgos?"

"Damned if I know."

"Tourists get weirder every year."

The next morning I set off running with goodwill toward men in my heart. Ready to greet the villagers. The men at the *kofeneion* see me.

"For the love of Christ, Yorgos, look. Here he comes again."

———

Hold the moment. As I said, my appearance was a bit of a surprise in the first place. Then there is the fact of my miserable language skills. During the night my brain changed *kalimera* (good morning) to *calamari,* which means "squid."

And then there was the problem of waving. I did not know that Cretans wave with a gentle gesture of an upheld, closed-fingered hand, backside out, palm in. I didn't know that the All-American hearty wave—arm extended, fingers open—is equivalent to giving Cretans the finger— "Up yours!" in other words.

To continue: Here I come. Running by the *kofeneion,* I shouted, "Calamari, Calamari, Calamari," and gave my most enthusiastic open-handed wave to all.

The Cretans heard, "Squid, Squid, Squid" and saw "Up yours!" From the priest in his underpants.

Well. They fell out of their chairs laughing. And shouted "Calamari, Calamari, Calamari" and enthusiastically waved "Up yours!" back at me. More than pleased, I ran on—thinking that these are truly friendly people after all—my kind of guys.

The men in the *kofeneion* could hardly believe what had happened. "What planet did he fall off of?" they wondered. And of course they did what you and I would do next. During the day they told their friends about the bizarre stranger's dawn appearance. And when their friends didn't believe them, they said, "It's true. Come see. Have coffee in the morning."

And sure enough, here I come again. I did notice that there were quite a few more men having coffee than yesterday.

"Look, Demetri. I told you. Here he comes. Shout 'squid' at him and give him the finger and see what he does." So they did and I did and so on. Funny, rowdy laughter all around.

As I ran on by, I turned and gave them the All-American sign for "OK"—thumb and forefinger forming a circle. They laughed even harder and gave me the "OK" sign back.

Wonderful!

Word gets around.

"You're kidding. No, come see." The next morning, even women and children were there to greet me.

But that same morning, just after I passed the coffee-house, a middle-school English teacher stopped me in the street. Serious young man, visibly upset. "Excuse me, mister, you are making a jackass of yourself, and those idiots at the *kofeneion* are helping you. You should all be ashamed. You are setting a bad example. What will the children think?"

"What's wrong? What have I done?"

"In the first place," he said, "no self-respecting Cretan man would ever go out of his house and into the village dressed as you are. Immodest." He went on to distinguish between *calamari* and *kalimera,* and explained the fine points of correct waving.

Finally, he wanted me to know that the sign for "OK" in America was the sign Cretans use for telling someone to stick their head up their own rear end. A road-rage gesture in Crete. A serious provocation that could lead to shots being fired. He conceded that good friends might use it as a perverse joke. But strangers? Never!

I felt bad. I glanced back at the men at the *kofeneion.* Sheepish grins. Now they knew I knew. And I knew they knew. And so, now what? I walked away puzzled: Should I leave the village, find another running route, apologize, what?

But I couldn't ignore one unambiguous fact: the laughter.

What had happened was funny. The laughter was real.

Actually, my best American best friends and I would have reacted in the same way. These Cretans still seemed like my kind of guys.

During the night my brain sorted out the problem.

At first light it was clear in my mind what to do.

I donned my running shorts and added to my costume a T-shirt with the blue and white Greek flag on it. Here I come.

Solemnly, the coffee drinkers watched me approach. No gestures. As impassive as the first morning.

"Look, here he is again, Yorgos. What do you think he will do now?"

"Is he angry with us?"

"Who knows?"

To prepare for this occasion, I had asked my landlord how to insult Cretan men in the way that's permissible only among good friends—the grossest thing—trusting they know you are kidding.

"Call them *malackos— masturbators*—and slap the palm of one hand on the back of the other hand, with arms stretched out in front of you. It is, shall I say, a suggestion of masculine inadequacy."

As I got to the *kofeneion,* I slowed down.

I stopped. Faced them.

A tense moment. Friend or foe?

I smiled. "Calamari." Then I waved, American style: "Up yours!" And growled *malackos* at them while slapping my palm against my wrist. To push matters closer to the edge, I made a circle with my finger and thumb. And stood there grinning, but with heart pounding—afraid I just might get the hell beat out of me.

The *kofeneion* erupted with laughter and applause. A chair was provided. "Come, come. Sit." Coffee, brandy, and a cigarette were offered. And with their minimal

English and my feeble Greek we retold and reenacted the joke we had made together—from their point of view as well as mine. Above all, they thought my way of handling the situation—the in-your-face-with-humor—had Cretan style. Arrogant. Only a true friend would be so audacious.

I was, after all, their kind of guy—and they were mine.

It seems there was an opening for Village Idiot, and I filled it.

That was the beginning.

For a long time they knew little about me except that I was a fool and a laugher who understood something about the humor and social courage of Cretan men. To me they became friends with names like Yorgos, Manolis, Kostas, Nikos, Demetri, and Ioannis. To them I became the *Americanos, Kyrios Calamari*—the American, the honorable Mr. Squid.

As I say, I have been going back for more than twenty years. They have included me in the life of the village— feasts, weddings, gossip, baptisms, wine-making, and olive harvests. My clumsy Greek amuses them still.

I return each year in part because I expect laughter— from their timeless jokes and stories that are often raw and reckless and wicked. Jokes about old age and sex and war and stupidity—jokes that mask fear and failure and foolishness. Their laughter is not cautious. Without this laughter the Cretans would not have survived their travails and tragedies across the centuries. Cretan laughter is fierce, defiant laughter—an "Up yours!" to the forces of death and mystery and evil.

They have a word for this laughter: *Asbestos Gelos.*

(As-bes-tos yay-lohs) A term used by Homer actually.

It literally means "Fireproof laughter."

Unquenchable laughter. Invincible laughter.

And the Cretans say that he who laughs, lasts.

And they have been around a long, long time.

47

Being There

Crete. Spring. The fine kind of day that called me to take the long way home from a shopping trip to the nearby town of Chania. Away from the seaside road, up through the coastal hills, on through a rocky gorge to the village of Vrissos, and all the way up to the edge of the mountain snow. The road was new and relentlessly switch-backed on a bearing farther east instead of west. Not a way home for me.

I was lost. On a road that was not on my map.

Coming to a small village I stopped across the road from an old man leading an old goat—(or an old goat leading an old man—it was hard to tell who was in charge or if it mattered to the man or goat).

I got out of the car and called across to the old man:

"Poo ee-meh?" ("Where am I?")

The old man and the old goat considered me with puzzled amusement: "What kind of question is that?"
Kindly, slowly, as if speaking to a child or an adult with
mental limitations, the man pointed to where I stood
and said:

"*Leepon, eh-kee.*" ("Well, you are over there.")

Carrying my map with me I went across to stand beside
the man and his goat. "*Oshee, oshee. Poo ee masteh?*" ("No,
no, where are WE?")

With amused pity the man considered me. Placing one
hand on my shoulder and pointing at the ground with the
other, he tenderly explained:

"*Ee-thoh.*" ("We are here.")

Yes.

I showed him my map. I indicated the empty space where
the village and the road should be. I showed him my
route—with no road. He scratched his head—this man
who probably knew every dirt track, donkey path, and
gully in this mountain valley—and asked me with amused
vexation:

"*Keh poo to vreekehs?*" ("Where did you get this map?")

"Athens."

He laughed. *"Athena?"* He laughed and laughed. He said "Athens!" in a way that implied they know nothing useful in Athens—they do not know where they are or where we are. The classic Greek democratic disdain for authority. The old man re-explained all this to his goat. And laughed. Even the goat looked amused. Clearly I was a hopeless case.

So I thanked him and went back to my car.

"Poo pas?" ("Where are you going?")

"Then-kseroh." ("I don't know.")

The old man laughed again. He smiled and waved and began talking to the goat as if to explain that this was the first thing I had said that made sense. If I didn't know where I was, how would I know where I was going?

Obvious.

Neither he nor his goat is lost.

They are there.

48

Olympics on
a Smaller Scale

*"It is not the size of the stadium that counts,
but the spirit of the play." So said the philosopher,
Epictetus, in the first century AD.*

Although verifiable records only go back to 776 BC, the Olympic Games have been a part of Greek life since there were Greeks. And it remains easy to enter into the Olympic sporting spirit. Like last night.

Some Cretan friends and I drank a fine wine. A dark, almost black, red wine—Aghiorghitiko grapes from Nemaea in the Peloponnnese region, near Corinth. In a playful spirit after a glass or two, we were inspired to initiate the first Greek Bug Olympic Games.

The main event was the Rolling-Down-Hill-and-Walking-Away contest. Each one of us found one of those little fast-crawling armored pill bugs. We touched them gently to make them roll up into a ball, and then using a piece of paper, scooped them up, held them in line at the top of an inclined cookie sheet, and let go at the count of three. The bugs rolled down and out onto the stone floor. The first bug that got up and walked away was the winner.

Place your bets!

My bug, Hercules, won five times in a row. A Gold Medal Bug. I went to find a very tiny olive leaf to crown the victor, but by the time I got back he was gone—too shy for the glory, I suppose. Humble bug. Class act.

Hercules reigns! Wherever he may be.

Harmless fun in the spirit of competition, which pervades all Greece this weekend. These small-scale Olympics were a warm-up for tonight's big event. All Greece will shut down at 8:30. The two top soccer teams will go at it in Athens. Panathinaikos and Olympiakos Piraeus. If you are not there in front of the TV, you will have nothing to talk about in the village tomorrow.

If the Turkish air force attacks Greece tonight between 8:30 and 10:30, the prime minister will say Greece cannot come to fight right now, but in two hours, half of Greece will be really mad and ready to kill, so maybe the Turks should pick another day.

Saying it's only a soccer game is to misunderstand how seriously Greeks take any sporting contest, small or large. I went off with my friends to the *Argentina Taverna* to support the local favorite, Panathinaikos. I tried not to step on any Olympic Bug competitors as I went out the door.

Afterward. A 2–2 tie. Sufficiently satisfying to all because the game was played hard and well, with elegant passing and footwork. Beautiful! Everybody won.

Epictetus would have been pleased. As he said, speaking of skillful ballplayers: *"None of them considers whether the ball is good or bad, but only how to throw it and catch it. For where a man has proper reason to rejoice, his fellow men have proper reason to share in that rejoicing."*

49

Irrational Actions and
Incoherent Utterances Experienced
During Oracular Ceremonies
of Prophetic Importance

The ancient Greeks had a single word for that: *klidona*.

And *Klidonas* is the name still given to midsummer celebrations around the Feast of Saint John the Baptist, June Twenty-fourth, which coincided with last week's summer solstice.

In the Old Days the festivities began the evening before, with bonfires in village squares. Music, dancing, singing, and the drinking of wine prevailed. The dried wreaths of flowers that had been collected on the First of May, were thrown into the fires. As the fires burned down, everyone jumped over the embers, while making wishes. The jumping was done in couples or with close friends and family. Afterward, some of the ashes were taken home and scattered around the front doors of homes. These are the rituals of fortune and magic.

For the same celebration unmarried young women of the village would bring water from a special well—never speaking while collecting and carrying the water. It was poured into smaller water jugs, into which each maiden put a *rizikari*—a personal item of value—a charm. And during the night they might dream of the man they would marry. In the morning each girl took a sip of the water, and after that, the first male name she heard was supposed to be the name of the man she would marry.

That was then. In the Old Days.

But now? Seeking a remnant of former times, I went on Saint John's Eve to the village of Drapanias. An agricultural village in the flat coastal plain of Kissamos at the western end of Crete. I was the only foreign tourist. But a welcomed one: "Come, sit, eat, drink . . ."

The event had the ambiance of an affair sponsored by an American PTA or a Lion's Club social committee. Just good-willed amateurs doing community service. Mostly local farmers and fishermen and housewives gathered in the village schoolyard. Ordinary people still honoring what had gone on forever on Midsummer's Eve.

The main attraction was a *montinades* competition. Each person put something small and personal in a basket. Then poems were recited or composed in a traditional

Cretan form—two fifteen-syllable lines that rhyme. About anything: life, village gossip, hopes, and dreams—even politics. But most often about love and desire.

"It's Cretan rap," I thought.

After each poem was recited, someone picked an item out of the basket, and its owner was considered the subject of that poem. If a handsome young man called out two lines confessing the power of his passion for his true love, and the item pulled out of the basket belonged to an eighty-year-old widow woman, the audience howled. And this can go on for hours—as it has gone on for centuries.

When the *montinades* event ran out of steam, a men's chorus stood out in the road in the darkness and sang ancient shepherds' songs in a haunting call-and-response style. The chorus was followed by children in costume performing Cretan line dances, backed by a three-piece band of lute, fiddle, and guitar. Finally, after consuming piles of food and jugs of wine, everybody wandered off home by the light of a full moon.

Though I looked carefully, I did not see any young women hauling water around as in the past. In fact, there was a notable shortage of maidens. I was told that most of them had been lured away by the young men to drink beer on the beach. No doubt still within the *klidona* tradition—"irrational actions and incoherent utterances experienced during oracular ceremonies of prophetic importance."

50

Not Even Chickens

With all the recent seaside development, it is easy to forget that Crete and Cretans are fundamentally about the mountains—the steep places, the high and isolated villages that breed independent, self-sufficient people who have always been a rule unto themselves. They still are. The Mountain Cretans say they fear nothing and nobody, and would look at God, Himself, with hat on and eyes open. Thus they look upon strangers with interest, not suspicion.

One afternoon I parked my car and walked a narrow road that connects several small villages along a high mountain ridge. A voice called out from the porch of a whitewashed house:

"Ehla, ehlah, kahtheeseh!" (Come, come, sit!) An old man beckoned to me, pointing to the chair beside him.

I went. I sat. On a small table were almonds, raisins, olives, and a bottle of *tsikoudia* (tsee-koo-di-ah)—the

Cretan equivalent of white-lightning or grappa—the prof-fered sign of hospitality and welcome to a Cretan home. He was expecting company—and anybody would do.

"Tho-kee-maseh" ("Drink this, eat this!") he said, hand-ing me a glass of *tsikoudia* and filling a small plate with almonds, raisins, and olives.

"Lee-pon. Germanos?" ("Well, then, are you German?")

I was touched to know that the hospitality came first, even though I might be German—from a country that had brutalized Crete in WWII.

"Oshee, Americanos." ("No, American.")

"Americanos! Americanos!" He shouted into the house, and a younger man appeared. They spoke high-gear Greek with a Cretan accent. The look on my face tells them I cannot follow, so the younger man says in fine English, "My father is excited to meet you. He has never met an American. He hears that in America they have everything. He would like to ask you some questions."

Fine. With his son translating, the examination began.

How old was I? How many children? How much money do I make? Very Cretan inquiries. Then a harder question that led to even tougher scrutiny: "How often do you dance and sing and recite poetry?"

"Not very often."

The old man looked at me with narrowed eyes.

"How many sheep and goats do you have?"

"None."

The old man looked puzzled.

"How many olive trees do you have and how much oil put away?"

"None."

The old man frowned.

"How many vines do you have and how much wine put away?"

"None."

The old man was nonplussed. He raised his eyebrows.

"Do you have any chickens?"

"No."

The old man looked mildly outraged and fell into high-gear Greek again with his son. The son was apologetic. "Pardon me, but my father says that it is a lie that Americans have everything. You have no sheep, no goats, no trees, no oil, no vines, no wine, not even chickens. He asks, 'What kind of life is that?' He says, 'No wonder you don't sing or dance or recite poetry very often.' He is dismayed."

The old man peered at me with pity bordering on contempt.

Shaking his head in disgust, he mumbled in English, as he rose and limped out into his garden, dismissing me from his mind:

"Nothing. Not even chickens . . ."

51

Liturgical Laughter

"Do you know any good jokes?"

Usually a reasonable question at an all-male con-
vivial social occasion.

However.

To ask that of a bishop of the Greek Orthodox Church
at Sunday lunch at his own table is risky. His Eminence,
the *Dispotis* of Chania, slowly turned his pale, white-
bearded face to me, gave me his Blessed-Are-the-Meek
look, smiled thinly, and went back to dissecting the small
broiled pink fish on his fine china plate.

(Silence.)

No, I guess he doesn't know any jokes. And that's
funny.

Here is a man sitting as host at a fine Sunday feed,
dressed in a long black dress, with glitzy-gold jewelry
around his neck, and on his head a stovepipe with a lid
on it.

I don't mean to be disrespectful, but I would think you'd have to have a sense of humor to dress like that at lunch. But he doesn't know any jokes. Yet he's so close to a good laugh. All he needs is a red rubber nose on his schnoz and a mirror.

Make no mistake—I like and respect this man, and we are friends. And I know I'm being irreverent. Bear with me a little farther.

I remember seeing his fellow bishops in full-dress Byzantine liturgical finery walking in a solemn High Occasion parade in Athens. Gold accessories, great bulbous jeweled crowns, and sunglasses. They could have been majorettes for a Gay Pride marching band. "Mother Manolis and the Saloniki Queens." Bing Bang Byzantine Bling!

Funny. At least to me, a foreigner, a heretic and heathen by official Orthodox standards.

And I know I'm way out on a limb here laughing at what is deadly serious business in a religious institution not my own. But that's exactly the point I want to address. Deadly seriousness. The lack of laughter.

Another guest at the bishops' luncheon, a visiting Roman Catholic parish priest from New Jersey, dressed incognito in jeans and T-shirt, asked me if I had a book in mind that I had not yet written. Yes. One on the humor of Jesus, "Jesus' jokes," I said.

"But there aren't any Jesus Jokes in the Bible."

"Right. That's the problem. My book would be about the missing material." And since Father William seemed open to the subject, I explained.

First of all my credentials. I am a seminary-trained, ordained Unitarian Universalist clergyman with forty-five years' experience in religious circles. Second, I am a man, with sixty-eight years on the job. It is biblically sound to say that Jesus was also a man—no less. A whole human being. Like the rest of us. He ate, wept, got angry, and bled.

And surely, surely he laughed.

We know he went to a wedding and provided wine when the reception ran dry. And he must have had the common cold, gone to the toilet, itched, and ached, and got hungry. Like the rest of us. True, not all of that is mentioned in Scripture. But it could have been. It should have been.

Moreover, he was the son of a working class, blue-collar family, with no formal education. He hung out with a close group of guys—fishermen and carpenters and the common riffraff. He was Jewish. He told great stories—some of them must have been funny.

So how could we think Jesus did not laugh—did not see the humor in this life? Otherwise his humanity is incomplete. You can't tell me that joy, delight, and the all-out belly laugh were not as much a part of him as they are of us.

Heresy? No. Absolutely not. Sound theology.
So, what happened to his funny stories? The human comedy?
The jokes got cut by the copy editors and censors along the way.
Monks and theologians and scholars and Inquisitors.
Those whose black dress shrouded their minds as well.
Religion became too serious to underwrite humor.

Here in Crete I am surrounded by Greek Orthodoxy. Greece is a theocratic state. Out of my great respect for the traditions, I often attend the liturgy in the local monastery and find it deeply moving. But it's a solemn affair, more like a funeral than a celebration. There is no laughter whatsoever in it. Never.

This troubles me.

If I am ever in charge of the matter, there will be jokes in the Scripture and laughter in the sanctuary—for what else is laughter but sanctuary from the vicissitudes of life?

And the priests will wear workman's overalls and carry hammers and nails and pliers and screwdrivers and wrenches—as emblems of those who are committed to constructing a viable society and building a better world. They will know how to use those tools, too.

And they will be expected to know the best jokes and laugh often.

"Good luck on your book," said my bemused Catholic friend.

"If it sells, I'll do the next one on the jokes the Buddha told."

"I don't think I'd publish the humor of Mohammed, though," he said.

"Well, yes, that could set off the Great Joke Jihad."

On the wall of my study in Crete and in Seattle there is a framed pencil drawing of a man—bearded, long-haired, with strong Semitic features and rough workman's hands. He's dressed in the ordinary clothes of his time—two thousand years ago. This is an image of Jesus. Not an icon— a man.

He's not just smiling. His head is thrown back in a great laugh.

The drawing is not titled. But nobody ever asks me who it is.

They seem to know. They like what they see.

They would love to be in on the joke.

52

Epictetus and Plumbing

"Happiness and freedom begin with a clear understanding
of one principle: Some things are within our control,
and some things are not."

Epictetus speaking again. Stoic philosopher, from
the first century AD.

My sewer system got plugged up and then began backing
up. Damn!
This is Fulghum speaking from the twenty-first century
AD.
I wonder if old Epictetus ever had to ream out a sewer?
How might he have applied his philosophy?

*"Of course, there are times when for practical reasons you
must go after one thing or shun another, but do so with
grace, finesse, and flexibility."*

One does not call a plumber in Crete. A Cretan man is expected to resolve his own household problems.

"When something happens, the only thing in your power is your attitude toward it; you can either accept it or resent it."

My bathroom systems are interconnected, with all efflu-ent passing through a pipe that may be viewed down through a drain in one corner of the floor, which is there in case there should be some overflow from sink or tub or toilet. But what can go down through that drain can come up through that drain. Which means that if you take a shower, you can emerge to find all the bathwater running out the bathroom, down the stairs, and into the living room. Where there are guests, now moving to the front porch.

"Every difficulty in life presents us with an opportunity to turn inward and invoke our own submerged resources. Try not to merely react in the moment. Pull back from the situ-ation. Take a wider view; compose yourself."

"Don't be alarmed," say I, slopping through the stream with a towel around my waist. But the guests are out on the porch because the toilet at the other end of the house has also backed up and overflowed. It's not just bathwater.

"Watch for how you can put certain aspects of an event to good use. Is there some less-than-obvious benefit in the event that a trained eye might discern?"

"Oh, well, then. This is going to be a nasty mess. Why don't all of you go away for a while and the plumber and I will sort things out." Alone at last.

"Once you have deliberated and determined that a course of action is wise, never discredit your judgment. Stand squarely behind your decision. Chances are there may be people who misunderstand your intentions and who may even condemn you. Take a stand. Don't be cravenly noncommittal."

"But we can help."
"No. Go away."

"Everything has two handles; one by which it may be carried, the other by which it can't. Grasp the right handle, or you will become bitter."

———

So, to work. Using all the towels, a broom, the mop and bucket, and bringing a hose into the house, the worst got washed away down the stairs and down the driveway and into the bushes. With the guests standing at a distance, shouting advice.

"Go away!" I shout. Way far away—like into the village.

"The life of wisdom is a life of reason. It is through clear thinking that we are able to properly direct our will."

Now the obvious task is to unjam the plumbing. The usual tools: plunger, coat hanger, broom handle, garden hose. Nothing. So, a trip to the hardware store, waving confidently as I pass my guests parked at the village *taverna,* anxiously drinking wine and no doubt speaking ill of me.

"Never depend on the admiration of others."

The Cretan version of Drano is something called "Mr. Muscle"—the only English words on the large orange bottle. The elaborate Greek instructions on the back are accompanied by illustrations. One shows that you pour the stuff down the drain. Another shows the drain instantly being scoured clean. And a final illustration suggests that if you get the stuff on your hands or feet, you will lose your fingers or toes.

"Nothing truly stops you. Nothing truly holds you back. For your own free will is always within your control."

Nothing suggests how much Mr. Muscle is required. And if a little bit of goo is good, a whole lot of goo must be even better, right? There was room for the whole bottle. Quiet. And suddenly, from somewhere deep in the system came BANG! BANG! BANG! Smoke and a gurgling blue foam rose up from out of the floor and headed my way.

"We cannot choose our external circumstances, but can always choose how we respond to them."

Run, jackass, run!

———

"The wise and good person is he who achieves tranquility by having formed the habit of asking on every occasion: What is the right thing to do now?"

So I slammed the bathroom door and walked out of the house and down to the *taverna*. Wine time.

"Those who pursue the higher life of wisdom, who seek to live by spiritual principles, must be prepared to be laughed at and condemned by friends. Never live your life in reaction to these diminished souls. Be compassionate toward them, and at the same time hold to what you know is good."

Wine with friends in a *taverna* is good.

"Generally speaking, we are all doing the best we can. Forgive yourself over and over again. Try to do better next time. When you know you've done the best you can under the circumstances, you can have a light heart."

And I called my Cretan friend, Nikos, who came and did whatever needed doing, including making the smoking blue foaming goo go away. Tranquility reigned in the house when I returned.

"Practice having a grateful attitude and you will be happy. If you take a broad view of what befalls each person and appreciate the usefulness of things that happen, give thanks."

Thanks be to Mr. Muscle, Nikos, and Epictetus.

53

In the Flow of
the Mud and the Light

A Greek couple—dear friends of mine—made their first baby this year. "Come look," they said. I looked. What could I say? Most babies look like Winston Churchill without his cigar. Even the best ones look like Winston Churchill after a face-lift. This one looks like the daughter of Barbie and Ken. Perfect. That's what I told the parents. Men usually say, "Beautiful." Women usually say, "Cute." But I get very high points for saying, "Perfect." And not mentioning Winston Churchill.

I wondered what the baby thought when it stared back at me? *"My God. Another big weird-looking thing. Are they all this ugly?"* No wonder babies scream and cry a lot.

I didn't know this baby's name. A Greek child does not have a formal name until it is baptized. And that event takes place somewhere between one and two years of age. A child is carried into the church, stripped naked, handed over to the priest—a stranger in a black dress—

and lowered into a tepid bath. The child is usually terrified, goes red and rigid, screams, and often pees. Much to
the amusement of the Greeks. It's not as bad as it seems.
It's worse. I have been a witness. I tell you what I saw.

Ah, but what right have I to speak critically of such
things? Me, a heathen, heretic, and certainly neither Greek
nor Orthodox.

I speak as an insider. Once upon a time, I was baptized.
According to the rules of the church of my childhood. Not
sprinkled like the Methodists, as if you were going to be
ironed. Not just dipped in an indoor pool for the sake of
convenience. Baptized according to Scripture—outdoors
in a river, following the example of John the Baptist and
Jesus.

My mother was a serious Southern Baptist. And her
cousin from Muscle Shoals, Alabama, urged her to take
no chances and do it right. The cousin, it seems, was a
"Two-seed-in-the-spirit, Foot Washing, Flowing Water
Baptist." When she sang the old hymn, "Shall We Gather
at the River", it wasn't about a picnic.

The summer I was twelve, dressed in white shirt and
pants, I was properly baptized in the Brazos River—more
formally named by the Mexicans, "Brazos de Dios"—the
Arms of God. My mother was pleased. I was not. I was
scared. My uncle Roscoe had told me to stay out of the
river because there were alligators and poisonous snakes

in it. But I lived. Was thereby "saved." And was told I
would therefore be going to heaven. When I tell the
Greeks about my baptism, they are impressed. Like I've
got a platinum membership card. An insurance policy
that can't be canceled.

> I don't believe one can save one's soul. I don't know what
>   that means.
> I believe one can only live one's life, saving nothing,
>   spending it well.
> But it's comforting to have my afterlife contingencies
>   covered.

And, should it prove to be the case that there is a heaven
and I go, I imagine my mother pointing me out in the
great golden hall. "Look, there's my boy, Bobby Lee! He
may have lost his mind when he grew up, but he was
properly baptized and so he gets to sit very close to the
front. The dippers and sprinklers and child-washers are
way back there—up in the bleachers."

Don't get me wrong. Baptism is a serious spiritual ritual.
No disrespect intended. As a metaphor for reawakening,
it can be meaningful if it makes you think about keeping
your path on this earth a righteous one. And that's a good
thing, no matter which religious club you join. There are
many ways. Some wet. Some dry. Some lost. Some found.

And if the Way works for you and for the commonweal, then do it.

The Great Law of the Conservation of Matter and Energy says nothing is ever lost. Everything is saved. Everything comes and goes. It only changes form. Water is essential to life. As is earth and energy. We exist in the flow of the mud and light.

That I believe.

54

Solstice with Nose Music

 The twentieth day of December.

Spring comes tomorrow for me.

The winter solstice is the beginning of my New Year. Even though the evidence of the change is felt only in the slightest increase in the length of the day, more light and life are on the way.

The weather gods have thrown a sinking curve ball this week, spinning wet North Atlantic air down across Spain into North Africa, warming it and bending it back across Morocco and the Libyan Sea, and curling it north again across Crete and on out over the Aegean Sea.

This is a Levantine wind that picks up perfume from the winter-blossoming orange trees in the groves along the African coast. Perhaps it is only the yearning of my imagination, but I swear I can smell this wind: the soft rain benevolently sprinkles orange blossom pollen across Crete. And the smell of the salty sea is always in the mix.

The olive harvest is finished, the trees trimmed and fertilized for new growth. More smells are added to the pungent air: the ripe note from the olive-oil pressing, the astringent note of smoke from burning piles of leaves, and deeper tones of fecund earth freshly turned beneath the trees to receive the winter rain.

Cretan nose music.

The sweet smell of distant irrepressible spring pushing its promise up through the winter of the spirit.

55

Winter Count

In this season of the year, the Audubon Society conducts its annual avian census. Worldwide, its members flock together to count birds. An admirable activity. In so doing, they contribute valuable statistics to ornithological research, while enjoying the social pleasures of gathering outdoors with their own unique species: Bird-watchers.

The custom of year-end accounting has merit. Financial reckoning. Counting one's blessings. Reviewing resolutions. Even taking stock of smaller, less obvious things and events may prove worthy.

In Crete there's a winter count in this category. Between Christmas Day and New Year's Eve, a count of the bugs in one's house is undertaken. It's a fairly recent tradition. In fact, this is the first year. And mine is the first house. I am the founder of the count.

The custom honors Saint Lethargius, patron of the

overfed, the bored, and the lazy. His followers gathered on the couch in the Chapel of Our Lady of the Inert yesterday afternoon, having postponed the meeting from the previous day, due to the disorganized condition of the high priest and his faithful acolytes. In that state we began noticing bugs. And started counting.

Oh, no—not bugs again. Yes. Bear with me.

Before long my companions and I were engaged in surveying the inside of my house and its porches, making our count, and recording our statistics. Here's our tally:

Scorpions-3—1 large ivory one—1 weeny red one—1 black

Spiders-3—all small; all brownish-gray

Moths-1—possibly of the Tribe of Clothes-eaters, now deceased

Grasshoppers-2—1 yellow, 1 speckled

Wasps-2—in winter dormancy, or possibly defunct

Cockroach-2—or maybe the same one seen twice

Millipedes-9—small, red and black

Centipedes-none—but we know they're somewhere around

Beetles-11—assorted sizes and colors

Pill-bugs-5

Snails-none living—3 small, white. unoccupied shells

Father longlegs-1—doing push-ups on the ceiling

Ants—maybe 30 tiny black ones and 1 large red giant

Cricket-½—with one leg missing - a partial cricket

Small snakes—rumors but no sightings

Too-tiny-to-identify-or-catch-but-definitely-bugs—9 or 10

Book bugs—little-bitty, fast-running eaters of literature—5

Flies-7 in three sizes—dead

Wall worms, short, red, rubbery—2

Unidentified tiny flying midges not seen but heard—3

Mystery bugs: Something that burrowed into the sugar
    bowl but was not found—1

Something in an apple—1

Something claimed to be in someone's underwear but not
    produced for objective identification—1

Factoid: There are more than seven hundred thousand known insects. So our count is shamefully low. We apologize. We will do better next year.

You may insist that some things we did count are not in fact insects. Don't get technical. If it's small, crawls, or flies around in the house, and tempts one to flee or kill, it is a "bug," according to the formal classification of our patron, Saint Lethargius.

And I share my daily life with these creatures. I dismiss them as "bugs" in the same way I dismiss unwanted plants as "weeds." But that's an ungenerous attitude toward amazing living things.

A sadistic member of our Investigating Committee urged us to put everything we could catch alive into a glass jar for a gladiatorial contest to the death. But that is a nasty Roman tradition, not Greek. Saint Lethargius is Orthodox. No. Too lacking in respect.

So we revived the Small-Scale Olympics.

There was a weight-lifting competition, using a coffee bean, a single popped kernel of corn, and a Cheerio. The pill bugs refused to participate, rolling up into a ball. But a red-and-black-striped beetle, when turned over on its back, defeated all comers by lifting all three items and tossing them over its head. Several contestants were, unfortunately, rendered *hors de combat* by the judge's inept positioning of the weights.

The swimming competition, held in the kitchen sink, was won by a black beetle. The cockroach won the sprint going away, leaving the scorpion spinning in circles, and the tiny ants wandering around lost. A spider ate a teeny-tiny-midgy thing on the edge of the pool, and the large ant carried one small ant away for lunch. The spider and the big ant were disbarred from further competition. Cannibalism is bad sportsmanship in any league.

A grasshopper that leapt from the top of the kitchen cabinet to the floor without harm won the Getting-Down-Off-A-Very-High-Place contest. Two pill bugs that fell from the same height remained balled-up, too stunned to move. Wrong league. Most contestants fled the stadium and disappeared as soon as they had a chance.

"Surely," you say, "This couldn't have really happened?"

Skeptic. Well, OK, the bugs were real enough. They were all there, doing their usual buggy things. We saw most of them. But all the rest of it? Well, of course not. Too much effort is required. The Society of Saint Lethargius has a cardinal rule: Never move off the couch.

But we imagined it could have happened.

And imagining that it could is the reward for membership in the followers of our patron saint. As he himself once explained, "If you can imagine it, why bother to do it?"

There were some things from that day I did not imagine.

Another kind of winter count.

That afternoon, alone as I floated down into the sink of sleep, I recalled the laughter of a friend as he got into his car to leave—still delighted by a small gift I gave him: a mechanical bird that barks every time you shout at it.

I recalled the farewell handshake of a friend with whom I do not share a common language—but he warmly took my hand and then pressed his other hand on top of mine as a seal on our unspoken friendship. He understood about the bug count. And will have tales to tell in the village.

I recalled the solemn ritual of an enthusiastic good-bye kiss on both cheeks from a four-year-old child who helped find some bugs.

I thought about the pleasure of having friends who are

capable of having such lighthearted fun on a dull winter afternoon.

I recalled standing alone out on the porch watching the countless waves on the sea, and then counting far away friends who I wish had been there for the winter count.

And I laughed when I remembered the pipe lighter my granddaughter gave me for Christmas—a little pink pig that shoots fire out his nose.

All of these things were real and true.

These, too, are part of a winter's census—nothing large—just the count of small winged things that fly through the air and perch in the heart and mind as memory.

These I counted. And slept.

Praise to Saint Lethargius, the patron saint of what counts.

56

The Story of the Leopard
in the Village and How Manolis
Learned to Waltz

Its once cream-colored body now blotched with a pattern of rust from abuse and age, and its backside now shredded with black holes from yesterday's shooting, "The Leopard" lies dead in the village square. The villagers lament its loss. And also dread the possible consequences. Willful vendettas are as unyielding as the stones of the Cretan landscape, and the killing of The Leopard could be the beginning of a cycle of bitter reprisals. Unless . . . unless . . . Young Manolis learns to waltz.

The seed of this story was planted in the fecund soil of young love when Young Manolis' aunt was wooed by an Austrian officer serving in Crete with the German army during the war. He promised to come back for her. Someday. The years passed. True to his word, he returned one fine morning driving a new cream-colored Volkswagen Beetle. The lady's brother, Old Manolis, the father of Young Manolis and the senior living member of the family, was outraged by the Austrian's presumptions and unrelenting in his refusal of the offer of marriage. The Nazis had killed his father. In the name of all the saints, *"Ochi!"* "No Germans! My sister marry a German? Never!"

With knives and pistols in their belts, Old Manolis and his sons escorted the terrified Austrian back to the night boat to Athens. They would not kill him. Unless he came back. They kept the Volkswagen, considering it a kind of war reparation, replacing the two donkeys the Germans had confiscated from their family in 1942.

Old Manolis did not really want a German car. He wanted a Cretan donkey. But he was persuaded by his sons to convert the tiny sedan into a four-wheeled beast of burden. Except for the driver's seat, the insides were gutted to accommodate pigs or goats. A metal frame was welded onto the roof to carry hay or fertilizer or bags of olives. And a hitch was added to the rear bumper to pull a trailer.

The car-become-truck was never driven on paved roads or into town because it was meant for work not pleasure.

And work it did—with the uncomplaining reliability of a slow-but-sure-footed donkey.

The vehicle's carrying capacity was truly prodigious. It was not uncommon to see the old man cramped against the steering wheel, the inside stuffed with three milk goats and a crate of chickens, rakes and scythes roped to the outside, a sack of cement lashed onto the hood, and the roof piled with a load of hay larger than the Volkswagen itself. When the roof load was covered by an army-surplus camouflage tarp, the tiny car looked like it was being mated by a giant tortoise.

And so it was, year in and year out, season-to-season, Old Manolis and the absurd little truck became a daily spectacle of village life.

Old Manolis came to cherish the vehicle and its sturdy utility, but he did little for it except to keep it running. When the front fenders rusted loose, he hung them back on with baling wire. When the headlights burned out, he cut them off the fenders and replaced them with flashlights. When the muffler fell off, he did not replace it, because now people could hear the cannon fire of the Volkswagen rumbling up the road and get out of the way.

And when great splotches of rust worked through the cream-colored paint, someone painted black circles around them, creating a wild-animal-skin effect. From that day forward, Old Manolis' car was called "The Leopard" in the village.

At ninety, when he became too blind and deaf to work or drive, Old Manolis *loaned* the Leopard to his oldest son, Young Manolis, making it clear that it was only a loan, not a gift. The Leopard would always belong to the old man. In a less traditional culture, he would have been buried in it.

But, now, alas, The Leopard's days are over. The shotgun's blast made a sieve out of the rear hatch, destroying the engine and the rear tires. Young Manolis did it. At age sixty-five, this steady, thoughtful, kind man marched out into the village square and blew his father's pet car away. His only regret was that he had no dynamite to obliterate the remains.

Why? First you must be told that Young Manolis' only daughter went off to Graz in Austria to attend university. Superbly intelligent, she wanted to become a doctor. She fell in love with a young Austrian medical student and brought him home to the village and her family. They approved. Even her grandfather, Old Manolis, did not object. Times have changed. This is the world as it is now. That she will marry a "German" is not a problem.

But there is a crisis.

It concerns the wedding reception. A thousand people will come to the celebration in the fancy hotel in Platanias: The whole village, all the relatives, and a mob of the groom's family from abroad as well. And on that occasion, the bride has asked her father—required of her father—begged her father that he will dance the first dance with her. Wearing a new suit and tie. Waltz. In the Austrian manner.

Waltz? Waltz! *Ochi!* No! He would not. Never!

His wife, sons, and cousins prevailed upon him. And worst of all—almost beyond bearing—his own father insulted him in front of his family. Old Manolis shook his finger under his son's nose. What was he afraid of? Cretan men fear nothing! Cretan men are dancers! The Germans would laugh at him if they knew of his fear. Crete did not win the Great War to go down in defeat over a dance!

The old man had done his homework—Young Manolis could secretly take lessons from the fat English lady in Halepa.

Young Manolis must learn to waltz.

Ochi! No! He would not! Never!

In retaliation, his father flung an inflammatory curse: "You are a coward!" shouted Old Manolis, and turned his back in contempt.

Ashamed and outraged, Young Manolis grabbed his shotgun and marched out of the house. He wanted to kill something. And so he did. BOOM! BOOM! The Leopard was shot with both barrels at close range. And now his father will never speak to him again. And his wife will cry for days, if not weeks. And, to his everlasting humiliation, his daughter will waltz with her father-in-law at the reception.

Forever after he will know what his family is thinking: "*Coward.*"

Unless, of course, Young Manolis goes to Halepa to visit the fat English lady and learns to waltz. He will. He must. Are not Cretans men? Are they are afraid to dance—even in the silly Austrian manner?

Of course not!

And, somehow, The Leopard will live again. The men in the village will see to it. Tires and a new engine are already on the way from Athens. The men will install a CD player in the car, as well. With a disc of the music of Johann Strauss already in place.

ONE-two-three . . . ONE-two-three . . . ONE-two-three . . .

Young Manolis must learn to waltz well.

He will be waltzing for Crete.

57

Megalo Paskha—*April 2004*

Suddenly—everything happens all-at-once.

Once day it is cold and windy and raining. And the Cretans are sluggishly enduring the last dull days of winter. The next day the weather turns warm, the sky blue, the land green, and the flowers explode from the soil. And the next day it is *Megalo Paskha*—Easter-doubled plus Passover—the rare calendar event when the Orthodox Church and the Western Christians and the Jews celebrate a holy day at the same time.

Suddenly—in the towns and villages you hear German, Italian, English, French, Italian, and especially this year, since Greece is a hot ticket—Hebrew. Four charter flights a day from Israel.

Suddenly—those Cretans who make their living from the tourist industry go mad trying to handle in one big week what is usually spread out over at least a month. The rental business rises like a high tide along the roadside from the town of Chania—cars, mopeds, bicycles, peddle boats, rooms, tours, whatever—and what is not for rent is for sale. Shops and restaurants that were shuttered and deserted last week are in full operation, and Zorba music fills the air all the way to town.

Opa!

Suddenly—there are lambs to slaughter and sweet breads to bake and clothes to buy. The churches and the monastery are decorated and everything that should be whitewashed is whitewashed—curbs, trees, walls, big rocks, and steps.

Between now and *Paskha,* the pace of life will intensify. Relatives are on their way already. The house must be cleaned. The garden must be tended. New clothes must be bought. Delight is the order of the season. And the only scandal is in not participating.

May no scandal be attached to my name!

Suddenly—it's midnight and the bells ring and fireworks are lit off and the feast is on. *Pilafi, horta, paidakia, kokoretsi, calitsunia, tsikoudia, wine,* and *fruita. Christos Anesti! Chronya Pollah!* Eat! Eat! Eat!

And how would you be certain you had taken part?

If you wake late on Monday morning from satiated sleep to find your pillow wet from drool, because your body has been too enfeebled to move during the night.

If your bedroom smells like grilled meat, mown grass, charcoal smoke, and the vinegary vapor of village wine.

If your jeans and shirt on the floor are stained with blood, soot, grease, tomato pulp, chocolate, yogurt, and strawberries.

If the pockets of your jeans contain shards of crimson eggshells, balls of gold and silver foil, and half a candy rabbit.

If the face you see in the bathroom mirror is blotched florid orange and pink and red, and the end of your nose, your cheeks and ears, and the back of your hands are swollen and sunburned.

If your eyes are bloodshot from smoke and wine in excess.

If your head feels like a baked pineapple and your tongue seems too big for your mouth.

If your hands sting when the soap washes over the many small wire cuts you got from clumsily binding a small bleeding lamb's corpse to the *souvla,* the long pronged steel turning rod.

If your wrists and elbows and shoulders ache from turning the *souvla* over the coals for three hours.

If your abdominal muscles hurt from laughing, and your stomach seems swollen as if you may never need to eat again.

If you cannot remember your real name, but you think it may be Yorgos or Demetrii or Kostas.

If the front door of your house is hung with a limp wreath of daisies, poppies, and wild rosemary.

If all the dishes you own and some you do not are stacked unwashed in the kitchen sink, and there are heaps of uneaten cookies and cheese pies and the cold charbroiled head of a lamb on the counter.

And if you feel awful, but you don't really care, because you know why, and it is a wonderful awful, beyond all sense and reason.

Then you have strong evidence that you have survived Easter Sunday in Crete with friends; that you have helped dig the pit, spitted and cooked the lamb, eaten the wild greens, sopped up the oil with bread from a wood-fired oven, lay on old carpets in the green meadow under the almond trees, chased small children around the fields, drunk far more juice of the vine than hospitality required, and laughed and laughed and then laughed some more before falling asleep in the sun, and somehow finding your way home, to fling your clothes onto the floor and your body into your bed.

You have been Eastered to the max, Cretan style. *Megalo Paskha!*

You will have done your part.

No scandal will be attached to your name.

And despite how you might feel before at least three cups of black coffee on this late morning after, you will know that it is you who have died and been reborn—in the countryside of Crete—not far from the deep well of reckless delight.

If Jesus does come back some glorious Easter Sunday, it will be here.

So declare the Cretans.

And then—suddenly—it's all over.

It is the Monday after *Paskha*—a day of recuperation for the Cretans and a day of return for the tourists. The ferries and charters haul most of the visitors away. Tomorrow the island eases back into a pace of *sigah, sigah*—slowly, slowly—from now till inevitable summer.

For all this *fassaria*—this general fuss and bother—ancient calmness remains. It is April. The blood-red poppies cover the hillsides here in this far end of western Crete. The monastery bells still mark the hour at six o'clock, followed by the baa-ing of the sheep trudging homeward along the road below my house at dusk, their bells binging and bonging as they go.

Small owls call as evening fades over the wine-dark sea and snow-capped mountains. A warm breeze wanders over from Africa and into the hills of Crete, spreading the usual perfume of orange blossoms along the shore. At dawn the fishermen will go out in small boats and cast their nets in the sea, as fishermen have done for thousands of years.

Wide awake in the deep silence and darkness of the post-*Paskha* night, I got up out of bed at three a.m. and went out on the porch to see if everything is all right.

For the time being, it is.

58

The Invincible
Ioannoulla

Tension pervades the atmosphere of my house this morning. I am uneasy. And my fellow housemates—bugs and snails and flies and spiders—seem likewise on edge. It is "Tuesday morning—condition red alert." Why? Because heading our way up from the village, with a bow wave of energy before her, comes the Invincible Ioannoulla, the keeper of the house.

A small, stout, all-terrain vehicle of a Cretan woman in middle life. Once employed for ten years in Germany where she absorbed High German values of sanitation and order, she now manages the domestic part of my life in Crete. While the bugs and I may occupy the premises, it is she who sets the standard of harmony, and she who maintains the rightness of habitation.

Dirt and disarray are anathema to her. Untidiness is a mortal sin. She does not believe cleanliness is next to godliness—cleanliness IS godliness. Weekly she comes not to clean but to cleanse.

Ioannoulla does not walk from the village. She marches. As one on a mission. She huffs and puffs up the last fifty yards and then the stairs, throws greetings ahead of her like warnings, and goes straight to the brooms and mops without stopping. Any living thing that does not wish to be swept up or washed down had better clear out, for the tarnished shall be polished, the wrinkled shall be made straight, and the rough shall be made smooth. Since I do not wish to be included in any of those endeavors, I go sit out on the porch while she works.

I do appreciate her tool sensibilities. For example, Iounnoulla believes the brooms and mops should be first-quality and readily available, not hidden in a moldy dark closet somewhere. I once considered mounting a new broom and new mop crossed over the fireplace mantel as a sign of respect for her standards. At her insistence I bought a brand-new, fire-engine-red Siemens super duper vacuum cleaner that can suck the laces out of your shoes. I am not allowed to use it.

I also appreciate her notion that all the bedding and towels and small rugs shall be hauled out to hang in the fresh air every week. To lie in bed at night on sheets and pillows scoured by the sun of Crete in May is to have an easy slide into sweet dreams. But first I must loosen the sheets, which have been tucked into a tautness that would please a Marine Corps sergeant.

Sometimes she comes twice a week—because she knows I have had guests who have undone her work. This week there was a red rain, which is to say a storm front cycled across north Africa, picked up part of the Libyan desert, smeared it over Crete, and then poured wetness down through it, leaving a fine thin film of rusty mud on everything. Without warning, like an ambulance corps, hearing sounds of a car crash, Ioannoulla arrived knowing I would be helpless in the face of this emergency.

"AFRICA!" she shouted, waving in all directions as she steamed up the hill. "KHADAFY KAPUT!" And she not only sucked up every tiny particle of dirt in the house with the *"electriki scoopa"* (vacuum cleaner) but also hosed down the atrium roof and polished all the leaves on the gardenia bush. That was yesterday. Today she has returned to do the more usual tasks.

She assumes I understand Greek. And sometimes I do. But at the speed she assaults me with language, I can only smile and agree. *"Nai, Nai, Kyria Ioannoulla."* (Yes, yes, whatever you say, dear woman.)

God only knows what I have agreed to. Though I suspect she knows I haven't a clue and only goes through the formality of asking me if it is OK for her to go ahead and do what she is going to do anyhow.

She treats me with the courtesy reserved for the feeble-minded and the inept. After all, I am a man, and even more deserving of pity—an American man. What would I know about keeping house?

I am, despite what she thinks, orderly by nature and have a strong aesthetic sense. I like flowers and fruit displayed around the house. I like having bones and stones from the beach sitting around in olive-wood bowls, and I like books out where I can see them and pick them up at random. I like my working papers and writing tools spread out on the desk for accessibility. And I like my shoes in a row by the door arranged by color. It is my style.

It is not the style of the Invincible Ioannoulla.

At the end of her weekly invasions the flowers are rearranged in one vase, as they should be; fruit is stored in the refrigerator, as it should be; the trash I've brought from the beach is moved to the back porch where it belongs; and books are properly shelved. All the papers spread out on my desk are neatly stacked together. My pens and pencils are put away in my desk drawer. And my shoes have been lined up according to weight, not color or utility.

We have not been able to reach an understanding or compromise on these matters. She seems to think that if she perseveres, I will learn from her example. This contest between single-mindedness and stubbornness has continued for several years and shows no sign of resolution.

Several times I have deliberately paid her more than she expects because she has delivered more than I require. She accepts the money. And then brings me a present the next time that costs more than the extra money.

I am now a Scotch drinker because of this habit of hers. I gave her twenty euro as an Easter present, and the next week she brought me a twenty-two-euro bottle of Scotch, such as she assumes a fine gentleman like me would drink. I hate Scotch. But she checks the bottle to see if I like her gift. Each week I have a little Scotch on the rocks at the end of her shift to show my appreciation.

I know. I could leave while she's here. But then I would miss seeing her astonishing performance of remodeling my house in four hours. And I would miss her farewell ritual.

When she is finished, she walks through the house inspecting, and then says *"Malesta"* with a sigh, meaning, "There now, it's the best I can do." She hangs her apron on the back of the kitchen door and comes to wherever I am sitting. Silently she looks at me the way a small child will— directly, unselfconsciously, considering me carefully, paying thoughtful attention to what she is seeing. *"Malesta,"* she sighs. And with a smile that mixes affection, pity, and blessing, she pats my face, winks, and turns away homeward.

It's not often in this life that I feel that someone has actually blessed me, but when the Invincible Ioannoulla says farewell, there is no doubt I am blessed. It's her last act of taking care of the place in which I dwell—as if she looks at the dullness on the surface of my spirit and knows, as I do, that it always needs a bit of polish. And the wink suggests that shining is on her list of things to do next week.

59

Two Weeks Later

I write in a state of frazzled contentment. The Invincible Ioannoulla was here this morning. Usually I sit out on the porch while she works, but today the dear lady arrived early under a full head of steam, a bouquet of carnations in her hand, announcing that today was *Megalo*—the day of Big Cleaning, because it was either the last cleaning day of the month or a minor saint's day, or the day after the Day of the Dead, or the house was in need of exorcism, or it was the Saturday before Pentecost, or all of that.

The "Why," wasn't clear, but the "What" was unambiguous.

The *Megalo* involves carting every loose item in the house out onto the porch—chairs, tables, rugs, and anything else except the beds. And this carting involves me, since the keeper of the house considers me to be a strong back with a weak-but-willing mind. The distinction between employer and employee gets vague here. And the work is done at her pace, not mine, which means a Cretan-style aerobic workout for me. Hup-hup-hup—up, down—in, out—hup-hup-hup.

Next comes a thorough sucking-up with the *elektriki skoopa* of all the smaller loose detritus, followed by a soapy scrubbing of all the terra cotta tile floors, then rinsing and mopping. She even brought the hose inside to wash down the walls of the atrium, which, fortunately, has a drain. While the floors dried, the Invincible Ioannoulla hauled the *elektriki skoopa* outside and vacuumed all the windowsills and doors. By now I was sitting way far out in the yard, not wishing to be vacuumed.

But I was in a fine mood through all this, because I had a surprise ready for the dear lady when the labor was done. In my freezer was Wonder-Working Raki Fuljumakis.

To explain: At the end of the wine grape crushing in the Mediterranean countries in late autumn, the *must* is left to ferment in barrels, and then distilled. A pure, clear, raw alcohol results. Italians call it *grappa*. The Turks call it *raki*. The Cretan version is *tsikoudia,* and they use it as a customary gesture of hospitality. A thimbleful is offered when a guest enters a Cretan home, and a thimbleful must again be downed on leaving.

This fiery little gut-bomb insures you are alert as company and alert on driving home. Many cultures flavor it, but the Cretans take it hard and clear and straight. It's not something I like or drink much of, but no Cretan would fail to offer it or fail to drink it. Any *tsikoudia* with any flavor added—especially anise—becomes *raki* by definition. It is not Cretan.

Ah, but Wonder-Working Raki Fuljumakis is another matter. I filled a clear one-liter glass bottle half full of *tsikoudia*, added half a bottle of holy spring water brought from the monastery community of Mount Athos, and stirred in a portion of wildflower honey from the gorges of Sphakia. Finally I crushed a fresh mint leaf and rubbed it around the cork. After being shaken well to mix, Raki Fuljumakis, was the color of summer sunlight, and its smell purred: "Drink me, drink me." I put it in the freezer to get it ice cold.

When Ioanoulla and I had put the house to right, and she had walked through saying, *"Malesta, malesta,"* I led her into the kitchen. Producing my frosty bottle of yellow light, I poured two tiny shot glasses half full, gave her one, and lifted mine in salute. "Raki Fuljumakis," I said.

Quizzically, with unfeigned skeptical tolerance, she took a sip. Then she knocked it back and held out her empty glass for more. The whole sweaty ordeal of the day's work was worth seeing the grin on her face. I winked. She winked. We had another glass. And patting me on the cheek as if I might have some good ideas after all, she went her way.

I treasure the memory of the grin on her face after her first taste. To be held in even mild esteem in the eyes of the Invincible Ioannoula reminded me of the times when

I got a gold star from an admired teacher in primary school for good behavior.

The Invincible Ioanoulla came back to say good-bye this afternoon. I am leaving for America and will not return for several months. She is a widow lady now, and times are hard for her. My going away diminishes her income.

Still, she believes that good-byes must be well done, and so she came to bring a gift. One she could not afford. A silver and amber *komboloi*—traditional beads—as a sign of respect.

"Thin berazi," she said at my protest. "It doesn't matter." It is the way she feels and what she wishes to do. She touched her hand to her chest and then to mine—meaning: "It is the Cretan way—from the heart to the heart."

"Malesta," she said. And patting my face one last time, she walked away, leaving me frustratingly mute. My limited Greek could not tell her what I will tell you.

I suspect—no, I know—she has no idea of the impact she makes on my life by just being who she is and doing what needs to be done and doing it right. Furthermore, she would no doubt find it strange that I would tell you about her or that I think of her as a guardian angel.

But if you wonder sometimes why I seem happy and content here, you would never fully understand unless you knew the part played by The Invincible Ioannoulla. Bless her.

60

Physics

My house in Crete is on the grounds of the Orthodox Academy of Crete. Despite its name, the Academy has become a conference center for cross-cultural communication and ecumenical interaction. When I am here, I attend the meetings that interest me. Just in case you might think we're sitting on our hands lost in theological Neverland, I list some of the lecture topics of this week's international symposium of physicists:

"Konishi Anomalies and Exact Superpotential of Non-cummutative Susy Field Theory" *and* "D-branes and SQCD in Non-critical Superstring Theory" *and* "Tachyon-Bubble Duality" *and* "Plasma-balls in Large N Gauge Theories" *and* "Structure Constants of Planar $N = 4$ Yang-Mills and String Bits" *and* "Three Dimensional Black Holes With Electric Fluxes." *Just to name a few.*

Of course, I don't know what they're talking about. That's why I go. And I'm not entirely in over my head. I

thought the last topic addressed my kitchen oven problem completely. And several times I've had thoughts in
line with some of the other topics after too much
Metaxa brandy. These physics guys are just talking theory. I've seen things. I know what these guys are talking
about. *"Alternate Realities?"*—been there. *"Loop Quantum Gravity?"*—absolutely. And I wake up in the fourth
dimension almost every morning. Sometimes I'm there
all day.

One question that remains hanging for me is that if
subatomic particles can be two places at once, and my
body is made up of subatomic particles, then why can't I
be in two places at once? I asked one of the physics guys.
He smiled. "We're working on that," he said.

It's inspiring to have these people around—mostly
young, mostly brilliant—from places like India, Israel,
Iran, France, Germany, England, France, Poland, and the
USA—just to name where the presenters come from. All
with their minds way out there and way in here on the
edge of a conceptual reality unfettered by ethnicity or
political boundaries. Only in the metaphorical sense are
there national black holes, but not in physics.

And theoretical physics is not all that's on the agenda.

I watched two young men and two young women
from the conference sneaking off together from the official dinner, flirting their way down to the village to eat
by the sea in the moonlight. Applied Biology. Now I un-

derstand what this afternoon's talk was about: *"Higher-Spins, Holography, and Duality."* Sounds like Cretan *kli-dona* to me.

Nothing new. Same as it ever was. Physical.

61

The Story of the Exhibition of the Village Underwear, or How Dimitri Went to War

Cretans are great storytellers. Heirs of Homer, they often interweave a central truth about human nature with the strands of their own experience and redecorate a good tale in each telling. Mythmaking is an ongoing tradition. A good Cretan village story is not the same as a published report of investigative journalism. Even Saint Paul wrote that "All Cretans are liars." Their biblical reputation makes Cretans laugh. With all due respect, they think Saint Paul would not understand poetry or jokes. I heard three different versions of the following story told about events in a nearby village. Who knows the exact facts? But it contains solid truth about Cretans' understanding of themselves— both the light and dark side. That part is certain. Adding touches of my own imagination to the story, I tell you what I've been told. You may judge how much truth is in it. You may decide to pass it on, with your own twist of imagination.

It seemed to Dimitri that his father had always been
mayor of their village. And that was as it should be, because he was a decent, dedicated man who thought public
service was an honorable responsibility—like his father
and grandfather, who had also been mayor before him—in
the Cretan tradition of inherited leadership. Dimitri, however, will never be mayor. Because of the exhibition of the
village underwear.

When the national government reorganized local political boundaries, many small villages were combined into
larger regional administrative units. In a contest with all
the other village mayors, Dimitri's father was elected to the
new post, and the reason people voted for him was because
he was so clever that his corruption was well hidden. So
they said. It was understood that any elected official did
business on a favor-for-favor basis. So they said. And the
under-the-table-way was the Cretan way. Since there was
no evidence whatsoever that he accepted bribes or cut
deals, he must be very clever. And a very clever mayor was
the very best kind to have.

Dimitri heard the gossip—heard the men talking in
the *kafenion*. "He must have a Swiss bank account."
"His brother is a dentist in Zurich. Of course." "That's
where the money for the new Toyota came from." "And
his wife has quit working—they don't need her income." "He kisses up to the bishop a lot." "And there's

all that money from the European Union for all those projects in the other villages. He must get a piece of that. After the army his son will go to some fancy university—you'll see."

But Dimitri had joined the professional army—as a career—because there was no money for university. The new car was his uncle's gift. And the only money the family had was in a Cretan bank, in a chronically over-drawn account. He overheard his parent's long, late-night anguished conversations about how to make ends meet on the mayor's modest salary now that his wife had been diagnosed with tuberculosis, now that the old house was falling apart for lack of repair, now that his sisters were of marrying age and there was no dowry or money for a proper wedding.

Dimitri seethed. His father corrupt? No. Never.

And not about to be, either.

Dimitri hated the village for its mean-spirited gossip, even though he knew that all elected officials were the targets of its small-minded slander. If you worked for the government, you were therefore corrupt. And the only reasonable response for a citizen was to be corrupt in return—shave taxes, barter for goods and services, do business under the table when possible, and lie when necessary. In other words, above all, to be clever.

Worse, the Cretans were proud of this. The Cretan Way. The Greek government had even cooked the books to get into the European Union, and when it was discovered, it was too late. "Why were they surprised?" said the old men in the *kafenion,* laughing. "They were dealing with Greeks."

But Dimitri was honest. As the son of his father, and his father, and his father before him, integrity was a matter of family honor. There was nothing he could do about Greek ways, but before he went off to war—to be a professional soldier for the rest of his life—he planned a small act of revenge on the hypocrisy of his village.

He was trained in the Special Forces for clandestine operations. With three fellow soldiers, he returned home on his first furlough just before "*Ochi* Day" the annual commemoration of General Metaxas's one word response to Mussolini's announcement of invasion and demand for Greek surrender. "*Ochi!*" No! And the Greeks beat the Italians half to death before they retreated from Greek soil. The village thought it symbolic to have the young Special Forces soldiers around for a few days at such a time.

There would be the usual parade. Everybody would gather to watch all the schoolchildren from the *demos* march through the village. Lines of miniature Greek flags had been strung across the main street and hung from the town hall. The night before there was a great *glendi* in the picnic grounds outside the village, with music and food and wine and dancing.

Sometime during the night, the lines of flags across the streets and on the town hall were replaced by strings of underwear. On display now were:

The gossipy priest's shabby gray boxer shorts, ravaged by age as if gnawed by dogs in the crotch from his constant attack on his itching behind.

The teeny-tiny pink-and-yellow thongs belonging to the self-righteous spinster schoolteacher.

The police sergeant's leopard-skin and zebra-striped briefs.

The magnificent flesh-colored bloomers worn by the widow Bakakis, she of the big mouth and even bigger ass.

And an assortment of the assertive padded bras worn by many of the village matrons and their daughters.

And so it went—strings of the shoddy and the flamboyant, the worn and the ambitious, the flowery and the stained—the underwear of the town displayed in all its truth for all to see. And speculate on. And gossip about. And claim, if they dared.

Now the village knew why there had been a sudden plague of thefts from clotheslines and the Laundromat. There was no pervert among them. Only an angry young man taking a parting shot at his village, waging war in his own way. He would never be mayor. But he was clearly successful at Special Operations. He knew how to fight with stealth—to hit where it hurt—and disappear in the night, back to the base in Maleme.

Well, they think it was Dimitri.

Nobody actually saw him do it.

Clever.

62

Grasshopper Mind

Crete. An August afternoon. Hot and humid. I'm hunkered down on my porch in a small patch of shade in a mindless stupor. Suddenly, from out of nowhere, a big yellow grasshopper lands on the sunlit stone wall in front of me, like a tiny circus acrobat suddenly leaping into the spotlight at center ring. TA-DAH!

Then she jumps again—about twenty times her length and about ten times her height, landing farther along the wall in front of me. TA-DAH!

Amazing. I feel like applauding. She's very good at grasshoppering.

I wonder what it would be like to be able to do that. The equivalent distance for someone my size would be about 120 feet, ascending to sixty feet at the top of the arc. A leap over a five-story building. TA-DAH!

If I could do that I would want to think about it carefully before doing it even once. Maybe once is all I would ever do it. Actually, I could do it. Take a running leap off a five-story building on the edge of a cliff. Nothing to it. The jumping part, I mean.

It's the coming down that would concern me.

Landing.

I wonder how it was the first time for the grasshopper on my porch. Some grasshoppers can also fly, you know. I don't know about her, but personally I would want to be one of the flying type.

I can imagine the novice grasshopper suddenly feeling the uncontrollable urge to push off. *"Launch! WOW, I'm really up here! WOW, I can fly!"* The grasshopper must have been immensely pleased—for a moment. I suppose there are klutz grasshoppers that don't get it right away and fly themselves into the ground and land on their heads, or who get so excited they forget to flap their wings.

I would probably be one of those.

I admire this grasshopper in front of me. Not only is she good at going up, she's good at coming down. She lands well. That's the whole secret of getting high and going far. Descending lightly. Landing well.

The day I graduated from high school, my daddy told me that I was too young to know what I wanted and not to be in a hurry to decide. He said success in life lies in wanting what you finally get—no matter what you think you want now or how far away or how high up you go. The goal is being satisfied with how you end up. Coming down successfully is the final test of a life. A grasshopper would agree.

Fifty years from now I intend that my grandchildren shall say of their long-gone grandfather:

"He went high, he went far, and he landed well."

63

"Bee-Yooo-Tee-Fool."

Tomorrow I am leaving Crete for Seattle.

Though I am still here as I write, I already miss Crete.

It's a curious thing for a child of the Texas plains like me to become attached to the people and culture of a Greek island in the middle of the Mediterranean Sea. No rational explanation.

But I suppose that in the midst of my own twenty-first-century life that often seems so temporary and shallow and confusing, I yearn for a connection to a deep-rooted place and deep-rooted people with ancient traditions that include unrelenting hospitality to strangers.

How surprising that I would wander so far and wide to find that in Crete, or that I would recognize it when I found it. Lucky me.

———

From my house I can see across the bay to a far hillside where the world's oldest olive tree has been producing for more than two thousand years. The villagers there have always taken care of it, with the same perseverance that they apply to taking care of themselves. They are a people who act with a generous care-full-ness that can encompass a foreigner like me. Whenever I visit their tree, I am given something to eat or drink, and some oil or soap to take away home. And always the blessing to "Go with God."

Cretan culture engenders rituals, and one of mine, when leaving Crete, involves a visit to Jimi, the village barber. His shop is a tiny one-chair affair tucked in between a gas station and a tire repair business. No sign—everybody knows where he is and what he does. One chair, one bench, one mirror, a cement floor, one barber, and a limited selection of the tools of the trade. No magazines or potted plants or background music. His shop smells of old-fashioned lavender hair oil and baby powder. Not exactly salon glitz, but Jimi is fast, friendly, and cheap. His haircuts last for three months.

A small, energetic, open-hearted man in his seventies, who often sings while he works, Jimi wears a white butcher's coat instead of a barber's smock. Why? Cheaper, longer lasting. Besides, he worked as a butcher for a while,

and the coat was still in good shape when he turned to bar-
bering, so why not? Men come to him for haircuts, not
fashion statements.

Jimi went out to Australia from Crete as a young man
to shear sheep. He stayed on to cut hair at an Australian
army boot camp for twenty-five years. He has one haircut.
For sheep or men. It's not only that my hair is shorter
when he's done, but my head seems slightly smaller.

Even so, my spirit is larger, having been exposed to the
essence of Cretan vitality. Jimi's Aussie/English and my
Yankee/Greek make for lively loopy conversation punctu-
ated with laughter. I've never seen him anything but ani-
mated, optimistic, and enthusiastic.

In truth, I ritually visit Jimi for a feeling I want as
much as a haircut. When he's finished, after liberally applying lavender cologne and baby powder, and whisking
me off with a soft brush, he holds up the mirror, touches
my hair and beard, and says "Bee-yooo-tee-fool!" "So Bee-
yooo-tee-fool!"

And while I may not actually look that way, it is the
way I feel.

No apology for my sentimentality about this island or its
people. Of course there are ugly places in Crete. And the
supply of the wicked and foolish and pig-headed is as
evenly distributed here as anywhere else.

And I am not a native, but always one who comes and goes—forever an outsider—which means I don't pretend to understand all that goes on day by day.

Still, after twenty-three years, "the soil of Crete is under my nails," as they say. And I am old enough to know that in this life you see what you look for, and you get what you are open to receive. And you belong to those whose company you cherish, for they will cherish you.

In my own limited, awkward way, I can say and feel deep down,

"*Eimai Kritikos*—I am Cretan.

"Bee-yooo-tee-fool!"

64

Intersection IV

Geography does not define the next set of essays and stories. Though wherever they may have been conceived, carrying them from one landscape to another improves them over time. What was begun in Crete has traveled with me to Seattle and Moab before it was finished. And the feedback I get when telling the same story to different friends filters out the debris.

I sometimes think of myself as a literary oenologist—a wine maker.

First, there's the soil and the planting and the caretaking of the vines in one place. After the harvest and crushing the juice of the grapes is left to ferment in barrels in another place. And some wines are said to improve by being shipped on long journeys and bottled at a final destination.

Along the way, many minds and hands are involved

before the juice of the grape is finally consumed as the daily table wine it's meant to be.

Likewise, many sensibilities affect my essays and stories—family, friends, and editors—each adding a creative step along the way. But it is the reader who finally completes the process with the additive of self.

This is brought home to me whenever a friend tells one of my tales to someone else in my presence. A new, improved, and enriched version always emerges.

To point this out is to risk saying the obvious.

But I want to emphasize the lasting pleasure of the companionship I imagine I have with you. How I would like to ask you some of the questions from my list, which begins on the next page . . .

65

The List

I have a list in the "active" pocket of my mind. A list I often refer to when thrown into the company of strangers while traveling. The list is labeled *CONVERSATION LIFEBOATS.*

It's the same list I use in emergencies at cocktail parties, receptions, potlucks, boring dinner parties, and my dentist's waiting room. I explain my plan to my unknown companions as an opportunity to condense the time usually needed to get acquainted—and a way to get beyond superficialities. Sometimes I offer them a choice from my whole list, and sometimes I just pick one item and go with it.

Here's my list. I'm showing it to you. Pick one:

1. Did you ever have a great teacher—in school or out? Tell me.
2. What would you be learning—if you had time?

3. What would you have learned to do if you knew then what you know now? (Another language, for example.)
4. What would you teach, if you were asked?
5. Teach me something. Anything.
6. Do you know any silly tricks? Coins, cards, face contortions?
7. If you could be an eyewitness to some event in history, which one?
8. If you could see anyplace in the world before human history—where would you go and why?
9. Who would you like to see naked?
10. Who do you admire? Who admires you?
11. Answer an unasked question—something you know but nobody would ever ask about and you would never volunteer.
12. Decisions of consequence—what forks in the road were on your Way—and what if you had taken the other path?
13. Pick another place/time in modern history—since 1700—to live.
14. Book, movie, you've read/seen more than once. Why?
15. What ability/talent do you not have but would like to have?
16. Ever thought about changing your appearance or identity? And?

17. If you were a spy, what would be your cover?
18. What was the worst/best summer job you ever had?
19. If you could know how your life will end but you still could not change it, would you want to know? Why or why not?
20. If you could live one short episode of your life over again—a day, week, month—which would it be? And why?
21. Do you remember your first love? Tell me.
22. Have you ever experienced the kindness of a stranger? How?
23. Do you ever have any bizarre thoughts? (I'll report on the unexpected responses to this in a later essay.)

The list is field tested. I've asked or had people choose to answer every one of these. The list changes—gets trimmed or expanded by what works or not. It's still not a sure thing. I've had people close their doors in my face—not willing to play. But most of the time I end up connected to astonishing dimensions of humanity. And the response to the list leads to topics I've never considered. There's no doubt whatsoever in my mind that:

Everybody has a story to tell and a willingness to tell it if asked.

Everybody knows things you don't know, but wish you did.

Everybody is a door into some other room in the world.

Anybody is capable of inspiring you.

Every situation contains opportunity.

A friend of mine simply waves and smiles at people he doesn't know.

More often than not, they wave and smile back.

Or ask, "Do I know you?" and he responds, "No, but you could."

The contact is brief, wordless, hopeful.

True, if you do these kinds of things, you risk something.

People might think you're simple-minded.

That's a good thing.

66

Talking with a Child
About Things

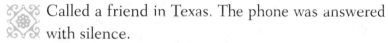 Called a friend in Texas. The phone was answered with silence.

Then, from a distance a deep male voice said,

"We have a plan. Now we need a gun."

Silence again. The phone was hung up.

What?

I called again. The phone was answered with a standard "Hello?"

"Jack, is one of your grandchildren around?"

"Yeah."

"How old?"

"Five."

"Does the kid like to answer the phone?"

"Oh, yeah."

"Are you sitting around watching the TV soaps with the kid?"

"Yeah."

"Did you just go out of the room to pee?"

"Yeah."

"Good. I had the impression you were planning a murder."

"What?"

Too bad I couldn't get the kid to talk to me. He would have, but his grandfather was probably too close by. Little kids who answer phones when their parents aren't around are great conversationalists. If you will only listen, they will talk and talk and talk.

And if you will reply to them as if they were real people and not stupid little kids, the conversation is often rewarding.

I recall the time I got a detailed account of the THING that lived under a kid's bed. Terrifying! Sure, I encouraged him. But nobody had ever asked him for an objective, clinical description of the THING before. The kid seemed to appreciate my sincere interest.

And he was just as fascinated by the description of the THING that lives under *my* bed. He was relieved to hear that the THING under my bed is old and slow and stupid now. No problem. I'm used to it. It's used to me.

I thought it my duty to explain to him that THINGS will be under your bed as long as you live, but they never ever hurt you. In fact, when they are old and feeble, they become amusing pets and sometimes retire to live way in the back of a closet somewhere else in the house or even move next door. They won't bother you if you stay out of closets that are not yours.

He seemed comforted.

"Your parents know all about this, by the way."

"Are there THINGS under their bed?"

"Yes. Are your parents home now?"

"No."

"Then go look under their bed and see."

"OK. Do you want me to call you back?"

"No. I'm Fulghum, the Federal THING Investigator, and I'm just checking. They know me. They'll understand."

"OK. I'll tell my mom and dad you called."

"OK. Good luck with every-THING. Good-bye."

67

Recollection While on the Way to an Appointment with an Opthamologist and Seeing Boys Choosing up Sides to Play Basketball, Leaving a Kid with Glasses Standing on the Sidelines.

We called him "Coach Price." He must have had a real first name. But the given name of an athletic director of junior-high sports teams is forever just "Coach." He was also team manager, team doctor, bus driver, referee, and mother-and-father surrogate to pubescent boys between the ages of eleven and thirteen—half too young and self-conscious to remove their underpants in the locker room, and half old enough to proudly wear their jockstraps on their heads in the shower. Mr. Price may have been the coach, but hormones ran the team.

One year Coach finally had a basketball team of promise. Five eighth-grade boys whose height and physical skill and intelligence had arrived early enough and settled down enough to make team play a real possibility. It was now or never, because the scrubs coming up from the seventh grade were still a long year behind in being anything useful on a basketball court.

And then there was "The Kid." The youngest member of his class, deranged by puberty-in-process, and legally blind without his glasses. To look through his thick lenses was like watching goldfish in a bowl. One eye wandered a bit. Without his spectacles he could barely see the basket, the ball, or the other players of either team.

The Kid did have his virtues. For one thing, he was determined to play basketball. He was small and fast, and when he dribbled down the court he had the erratic, unpredictable moves of an alarmed jackrabbit in full flight. Furthermore, he was a tenacious ball handler—unwilling to give up possession to any player, no matter which team they were on.

On the negative side, he seemed dyslexic in the face of diagrammed plays, reliably doing the opposite of any play devised. In short, he brought chaos to the court. And not even in practice had he ever put a ball through the net. He didn't care. He came to play.

As the varsity squad was trimmed of the truly inept, The Kid remained. He would not quit. And, to the surprise of all, Coach did not cut him from the team. Because Coach had a crazy idea.

For one thing, there were only ten players left. Without

The Kid, the team could not practice. But even more important, Coach began to see The Kid as a secret weapon.
The kid's vision-impaired eagerness could bring total
confusion to the court. If inserted into a game when the
opposing team was on a roll, The Kid might completely
disrupt the flow of play. Coach thought that, in a close
game, The Kid could be a living, breathing, fire-eating
psych-out—one-man myopic mayhem.

In the kindest terms Coach explained these matters to
The Kid and the team. He promised The Kid he would
award him a team letter and a letterman's jacket if he
would stay the season, whether he played or not.

"I need you. The team needs you," said Coach. And
that was more than enough for The Kid.

He redoubled his efforts in practice, falling on loose
balls as a Medal of Honor winner might cover a grenade.
His unpredictable play on the practice squad made the varsity team think hard about what they might face in a real
game. They called him "The Bomb," partly out of amusement, partly out of a mixture of contempt and respect.

Alas, he only practiced. He never played. The team
won without him.

But it was enough for him to know that at any moment
Coach might say, "Take off your glasses and go in and
drive them crazy." The Kid would have erupted off the
bench like an arena gladiator. Coach knew the other team
had never come up against a single-minded, cockeyed

jackrabbit before. He must have laughed whenever he thought about it.

The team won the city championship, defeating the other three junior highs. At the team banquet Coach declared The Kid "Most Valuable Player."

"You never played, but you never let us down," said Coach.

And The Kid never forgot that affirmation.

He was probably not the first or the last weird kid for whom a place was found during the career of Coach Price. The man had a gift for turning a loser into a winner. He had a gift for getting a team to appreciate oddball players. And he had a sense of humor.

With these strengths, I'm sure that many stories like this one could be told of Coach Price, but it's the only one I know.

This story is not about basketball.

This story is about great teaching.

It's about the imagination it takes to respect kids and find a place on the team, even for the least of them. This story belongs to Coach Price, and I've often wondered how he might have told it.

But I am certain of the long-lasting effects of the story.

I was The Kid.

I remember.

68

The Learning Curve

The Great Law of Unanticipated Consequences remains in force in human affairs, without amendment. It applies to all wars, past and present, for example. And things like DDT, free love, Play-Doh, Viagra, Super Glue, fertilizer, nuclear energy, and spray paint.

My first encounter with this dictum was memorable. As an eight-year-old Cub Scout on my first overnight outing. A Senior Scout had advised me to bring cans of pork-and-beans. No cooking pot needed. Just set the can on the fire. What do you mean I should have opened the can first? Who knew?

The explosion scattered the fire and the pork-and-beans and ten Boy Scouts over an astonishingly large area. And a night spent in a sleeping bag made sooty and sticky from the fallout tended to bring home the relevance of the phrase, "It seemed like such a good idea at the time."

(Of course we did it again. For years we did it again. Until a kid got hurt. The learning curve is not always steep.)

We often know what we're doing and even why we're doing it.

But we don't always anticipate what we do does or will do.

69

Headline Stories

Thoughts I wrote in my journal over one weekend, provoked by the headline stories shouting out about disasters from newspaper vending machines.

Stoic wisdom about death and destruction is always proportionate to your distance from the scene of the accident.

Sometimes somebody is to blame. Not everybody must be excused.

If you imagine that what you fear in the future is already part of your past, the present looks pretty good.

———

The question is not, "Is what you have sufficient?" but "Are you sufficient for what you have?"

There are many ways to lose your life. Death is only one of them.

"The body count is expected to rise," they always say. Yes. I already knew that. Everywhere. Every day. Forever. The body count will rise.

Reflection: How much better I would feel if I knew exactly how many avoided death and injury by an inch or a second, and then got up and pressed on. That's what I want to know. Who was lucky? Give me a count of those who dodged the bullet or walked through the fires of hell and lived to tell the tale. Remind me that it's possible to be one of those.

I know it, but remind me.

Whenever I'm in a European city like Munich or Athens or Rouen, I look carefully at all the older people—the ones over seventy. The survivors. And I think about what they've been through since they were young: repression, and occupation, starvation, brutality, bombs, disease, the death and dismemberment of friends and family, lost love, and the loss of everything but life itself. And they got up and went on with it. What difference did counting the dead make?

Count the living, I say.
    The unbowed, the unbroken, and the determined.
    And the lucky.
    And count me in.

70

Orange

This story belongs to Gussie Brock. We called her Gussie the Viking.

Long ago her Norse ancestors migrated west in open wooden longboats across the North Atlantic to settle in Iceland—ninth century. The restless gene in Viking blood must have remained potent because, when Canada opened its western prairies to homesteaders after World War I, Gussie's family left Reykjavik and immigrated to the province of Alberta to settle near the town of Medicine Hat on the South Saskatchewan River.

They dug in on raw land, built a sod house, and went to work farming. Harsh country. Mean winters. Hot summers. Relentless winds. Drought. Tough life. Hard times. Matched by strong people. Somehow they hung on. But just barely.

The family moved west to begin again—into the far northwest corner of the state of Washington where the land was better, the winters softer, the land richer, and water more abundant. Gussie grew up, married, had a family of her own, and moved to Edmonds, Washington. She was an active member of the church where I was the minister. When I first met her she was in her late sixties. Tall, slender, fair complexion, reddish-blonde hair. Energetic and strong. Viking woman, but not the barbarian kind. There was an air of good-humored dignity about her. We all thought she was the classiest lady in the congregation. As lovingly graceful a woman as ever we knew. So it was no surprise when she became an archangel.

Explanation:

One year, when someone noted that Unitarians don't have any saints, we decided to see if we had a candidate in our congregation. We did. And one Sunday, more as a piece of lighthearted foolishness than liturgical propriety, we elevated a member of our congregation into sainthood, because everybody recognized that Wilbur Saxton was a saint if anybody was. The best. (He died while I was finishing this book. The church was packed—standing room only. His halo was retired.)

One thing led to another, and before long we had installed another member of the parish as a deacon, because Marion Lewis clearly was one. And that led to the naming of Joan Anderson as an angel, because she was that.

And when the idea of having an archangel arose, there was no contest: Gussie the Viking, who was eighty that year. In solemn ceremony we declared her virtues, gave her a white robe, magnificent white feather wings, and a halo. The Archangel Gussie. She was very pleased. As were we, since not many people can say they know an archangel personally.

Now I well tell you her story.

But first, how I came to know it:

One year I asked members of the congregation to tell me Christmas stories from their lives. I would compile them into a Christmas Eve sermon. Many stories were offered. But one was so inspiring that it was the only story I told that Christmas Eve.

(I paraphrase Gussie's words:)

Well, you know, life was so desperate out there on the prairies, and we were so poor that the most we could ever expect for Christmas was to be alive, warm, and have something to eat. The worst Christmas of all came after a week of heavy snow. Firewood was scarce. We were burning dried cow pies for heat and huddling together in a heap under all our blankets in all our clothes to keep from freezing to death. We were living off boiled potatoes and turnips, and there might not be enough to last until spring . . .

On that Christmas morning my father got up and made a fire as usual. He was a solemn, stubborn, hard-working man. We knew he loved us, but like most Icelanders he didn't express his feelings openly. It took all he had just to keep us alive. But he did that with all this heart and soul and strength.

My mother was ill—too sick to get up or eat. When father called us kids to the fire, we didn't expect much—least of all any presents. As we crawled sleepy-eyed and shivering out of bed, we stopped, astonished. For there in the dim light we saw on the table—an orange. A single orange on a white napkin. We were dumbstruck. An orange. An ORANGE! Out here in the middle of nowhere in the middle of winter. An honest-to-God orange, glowing in the dim light like a golden ball.

"Merry Christmas," my father said, "the orange is for you."

How on earth did he get that orange? Where? When? How long had he had it? It was two days' ride on horseback to the railroad line. Three days to the nearest village. He was capable of doing something like that, but we wanted to know the exact details. We begged him to tell us. But all he would say was, "It's a miracle."

And we might as well believe that, because there it was.

We sat still as he so carefully peeled the orange and divided the sections to give each child an equal share, along with pieces of the peel. The smell filled the room. Our mouths watered in anticipation. We were almost afraid to touch the miracle in front of us. And then, oh my, what a moment, we began to eat the orange, the juice dripping on our fingers and down our chins. I can still taste it. The sweetest thing I ever ate.

My oldest brother suddenly said, "Wait."

He pointed at Dad.

We saw that Dad had given all of the orange to us, the children. Every bit. None for him. So my brother took a knife and cut a piece of his orange and placed it in front of my father. And the rest of us did the same.

My father divided his share in two parts. "These are for your mother when she's better," he said, and then we watched as, slowly, like a man taking holy communion, he ate his share of the orange.

It was the only time I ever saw my father cry.

As the years went by, the story of the orange became a family legend, told by generations of the family. We kids always said it was the finest gift we ever got. My father said it was not the same for him.

He said his best Christmas present ever was the moment when his children noticed he was without and gave back to him part of what he had given to them.

You know, he was a stubborn man, and he took his secret with him to his grave. We knew he had gone to a lot of risky trouble to surprise us. There was nothing supernatural about it. Our dad had done it. But no matter how hard we pled to know how he'd got that orange, he'd would only say, "It was a miracle." And I guess it was and will always be.

71

Breakfast

Common table salt is sodium chloride. One atom of sodium plus one atom of chlorine. It is the product of a reaction between hydrochloric acid and sodium hydroxide. (*Thank you, Mr. Science.*)

Fancy boutique table salt is the very same stuff, just different in size and purity and additives. Simply said, it's all sea salt. Either mined below ground from deposits laid down by ancient oceans, or else collected from evaporation ponds—with slight color and flavor differences depending on what is left in it—remnants of soils and algae and minerals and stuff.

Still, salt is salt, chemically speaking.

So then, you might ask, why do I have so many kinds of salt on my kitchen shelf? There's Kosher salt, *fleur de sel* from the Camargue region of France, black salt from India, fossil salt from Utah, and pink salt from Hawaii. I'm a sucker for salt.

Why? Answer: Poetry. Romance. Mental travel.

Just this morning I shook a tiny spoonful of Mediterranean sea salt over my scrambled eggs. Made me think of a trip I once made to the French town of Aigues Mort for the annual gypsy festival. The salt-drying pans are nearby.

In the same spirit, I used brown eggs, not because they differ from white eggs on the inside, but because brown eggs are beautiful. The coffee beans I ground came from Ethiopia. And the water I used to make the coffee is Evian—out of springs fed by French glaciers. The cream in the coffee was from cows that graze the Skagit River Valley in the Pacific Northwest. The orange juice was squeezed from mandarins just in from Japan. Irish butter. Lemon marmalade from Spain. And a shot of seven-star Metaxa brandy from Greece. (Good for the blood, my Cretan friends say.)

Sitting at my breakfast table I traveled the world this morning. My mind was beyond the horizon when I got up to go about another day.

Oh sure, the ingredients were a bit pricey, but it was cheaper than going out for breakfast. Above all, I set off into the dreary rainy day in a lovely mood, digesting memories that are salted away and preserved in mind and body and soul.

72

The Last Stages of Life and Why a Limited Opportunity for Lion Hunting Shapes Mine

In the Hindu tradition the fourth and final stage of life is the time to give away your possessions and wander around as a naked holy man. Or live as a reclusive hermit. In other words, when you're old and in the way, get out of the way. Not a bad idea, but not my style.

Quite by accident, an African approach came calling.

Having run out of anything to read, I browsed a neighbor's bookshelves one night and found a huge volume on the Maasai—the African tribe living astride the Kenyan-Tanzanian border. Exhaustive text and pictures and illustrations. A late-night read. What I found was inspiring.

In the Maasai tradition, the final stage of life is that of Senior Elder. I quote: "Admired and treated with great deference by all younger persons, the Maasai Elder looks forward to an old age not of isolation and fear but of continuing involvement in the life of the people." Yes. Better idea.

Furthermore, I learned that if I were a Maasai Elder, I would have plenty of cattle by now. Several wives would do all the work, including keeping the house tight and cozy by regularly smearing fresh cow dung over the walls.

I would wear elaborate beaded jewelry, coat my head with red ocher paint every morning, and decorate my ears with beads and bones. Around my shoulders would be flung a red-and-black blanket, with a red-and-white plaid sarong and a lion-skin toga to complete the outfit.

I would carry a white walking staff as a sign of peaceful intentions, and hold a fly whisk made from the tail hair of a wildebeest as a sign of leisure. Once in a while, on special occasions, I could wear my lion-mane hat or my ostrich-plume headpiece.

At all the dances and celebrations, I would be the honored guest, being the first to receive the best honey beer, the choicest cuts of barbecue, and the first gourd of hot blood from the sacrificial bull.

In the evenings I would gather with my fellow Elders to tell stories and discuss issues important to the tribe. The young would gather around us, knowing we are the conservators of Maasai legend and lore. The wisest among us would combine the qualities of a spiritual leader, diviner, keeper of the rituals, and healer. When we Elders sat together under a tree, the tribe would look at us and say, with pride, "*There*, in those fine men, is the heart and soul of the Maasai."

When I became feeble and infirm, my extended family and the tribe would feel honored to care for me. And when I died, they would wrap me in my finest red blanket, carry me some distance away, and simply leave me to be eaten by wild animals. No fuss, no bother, no problem.

The Maasai Way.

Of course, the Maasai are primitive savages. So some say.

In our culture it so much more civilized to be warehoused in an extended-care facility playing bingo, watching TV game shows, living in pajamas and old bathrobes, eating baby food, and being taken for rides to the mall in a little bus.

With no invitations to sit in the front row at the dance of the young maidens? Not even an ostrich feather headdress or a cup of hot blood?

As far as managing the final stages of life goes, the Maasai are way ahead of the Hindus or us. So say I. And I'm thinking of applying for Senior Elder status in the Maasai.

But, alas, I note that a requirement is to have killed a lion first to prove one's worthiness. There's always some fine print. Not a lot of lions in my neighborhood. And if I got caught stalking around the zoo with a spear . . . well, no. For lack of a handy lion, I am shut out of the Maasai Way and will have to figure out a better Way of my own.

73

Sock Epiphany

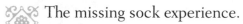 The missing sock experience.

"The washer ate one of my socks," we say.

Or "There must be a miniature black hole in the dryer."

Or "One of my socks escaped during the night."

There is another way to look at this.

A visiting friend transferred my laundry from out of my dryer onto the folding table, sorted my clothes, found one sock left over, and exclaimed,

"Look! Your dryer made an extra sock for you. When it makes another one, you'll have a new pair. You're not behind, you're ahead!"

Oh.

Well. Yes. A new view of the mysterious workings of the dryer.

Now I approach it eagerly anticipating spontaneous conception.

I need one more brown sock.

74

Secret Agent X
and Mothers' Day

My host for a speaking engagement had lodged me in a high-end hotel: The Ritz. The concierge desk was attended by two alert young men in frock coats, with the crossed keys of their profession pinned to their lapels. Sleek as seals—handsome Italianate faces right out of an Armani advertisement. Earnestly eager to assist in any way I might require.

But my need was mundane: a new leather band for my reliable old wristwatch. And a new shoestring for my shoe. If I had wanted to buy a new Ferrari, the concierges could have helped me right away. If I had wanted a private jet to take me to Dubai, no problem. If I had needed a table for ten to honor a Grand Duke, done. Have my mink coat cleaned in an hour? Of course. And tickets for any opera in the world—piece of cake.

But a watchband? For an old watch? And a shoelace?

One moment, please. Consultation in English, Italian,

and French—search of computer, Rolodex, and telephone books. Nothing.

A third character entered the quest: The classy young
blonde female front-desk manager, who has been moni-
toring the situation. "Marcel," she calls, raising her eyebrows. Marcel looks up. "X?" she asks. Marcel nods, "Ah,
oui, but of course. X." He writes a few words on a piece
of paper and passes it to her. He turns to me. "Please wait
a moment, sir. Have a seat."

Meanwhile, the young woman smiles at me, makes a
phone call, writes a note, and passes it to Marcel, who
glides over to my chair. There are two addresses and a
small map on the piece of paper.

"What you wish is nearby. Shall we send someone for
you or shall we make an appointment? Would you like us
to arrange a car and driver to take you?" If I had replied
that I wished him to carry me piggyback, he might have.
But it was a nice day, and I walked.

When I returned with my new watchband and shoelace I noticed that the concierge desk was vacant, so I felt
free to ask the young woman at the front desk, "I don't
mean to pry into professional secrets, but I'm curious.
Who did you call on the phone for consultation? What
did you mean when you said 'X' to Marcel?"

"Promise not to tell," she said.

"I will be discreet," I said.

"When all other information resources of the concierge
desk of the Ritz Hotel fail, we call my mom."

"Your mother?"

"Yes, my mother. Agent X."

"She's a retired schoolteacher, lives nearby, knows everybody, and is out and about in the world. We have not stumped her yet. I never realized how much my mother knew until I got this job. She's better than Google or Yahoo or Craig's List. Occasionally the hotel thanks her by inviting her to spend a night as our guest. I think of her as job security. We all refer to her as Secret Agent X. My mom never lets me down."

Happy Mothers Day to Agent X—and all her sister agents.

75

Bizarre Thoughts

"Ever have any bizarre thoughts?" asked the doctor.

So begins the title essay of the book *The Second Tree from the Corner* written by E. B. White, published in 1935. That book and White's *Charlotte's Web* sit side by side on my shelf of classics—books to be reread from time to time. Part of the pleasure lies in revisiting their author. White ranks high on my list of people I wish I had for a next-door neighbor.

The essay continues: "He was about to say 'Yes' when he realized the next question would be unanswerable. Bizarre thoughts, bizarre thoughts? Ever have any bizarre thoughts? What kind of thoughts *except* bizarre had he had since the age of two?"

My mind does weird things. For example, some nights when I'm half asleep I hear the doorbell ring. *Ding-dong.*

Ding-Dong. And I don't have a doorbell. But it seems so real that more than once I have stumbled out of bed and downstairs to the door to see who's there. Nobody. Again.

Here's the really bizarre part: Imagining who it might have been. What did they want? Wondering if I slept on the couch close to the door would I catch them the next time they rang?

On the way back to bed the music starts again. For the last three days the jukebox in my mind has been playing the 1978 pop tune "Y.M.C.A." by the Village People. I didn't turn it on. I can't turn it off.

As I sleepily climb the stairs in the dark, one part of my mind is muttering to another part: *"Stop it, stop it, STOP IT!"*

You, too?

I know I'm not alone. There's a relentless flow of twisted mental traffic popping through the raw meat between the ears of the most normal-appearing people. We get used to it, filter it, repress it, or ignore it. But seldom discuss it.

Sometimes I see the slightest fleeting smile cross the face of someone during a dinner-table conversation, and I know: A bizarre thought just sparked through their inner cave like the collision of quarks in a particle accelerator.

So why not ask? "Ever have any bizarre thoughts?" has become my party inquiry. When the small-talk and white wine and mystery nibbles have dulled the senses, and the glazed look that accompanies unfulfilled expectations clicks into place, I've asked.

The inquiree usually snaps to full alert. *What?* And I repeat the question—with an explanation, and a promise to tell them a bizarre thought of mine in return. Without exception, an uncontrollable grin appears. And we're off to the races. Exceptional samples:

The surgeon who wondered what human flesh might taste like.

The chairman of a board who imagined what all those attending a meeting might look like naked as they sat around the big table.

The minister who had an urge to begin a sermon with a dirty joke.

The nice housewife/mother who wished she had some magic mushrooms to put into her family's morning pancake mix.

The real-estate agent who considered burning down the house of a nasty client.

The schoolteacher who thought about showing up in class dressed like the Madonna.

The retired barber who makes speeches to Congress when he takes walks alone in the evening.

The woman who imagines what she would do if an Angel of the Lord appeared to her like they used to do in the Bible.

And this is just the tame and harmless stuff. There's worse.

Bizarre.

Makes my hearing doorbells seem trivial.

Of course, their confidence is assured by my agreeing from the outset to share a bizarre thought of my own. If I tell, they'll tell. It's my impression that the interchange adds a dimension of amused conspiracy to a dull occasion. "Normal" includes weirdness. Most of us just keep it to ourselves. A psychiatrist told me that most of us are crazy. Sanity only means we keep the craziness under control.

People like Robin Williams and Whoopie Goldberg and Phyllis Diller make a living off having bizarre thoughts in public. And we wouldn't laugh at what they say if we didn't recognize the loonyness loose in ourselves.

It may be that my ritual inquiry regarding bizarre thoughts will limit the number of party invitations I receive. *"Don't invite him. He's a nut case."* But maybe not. There's a fruitcake on the back shelf in most of us. There are no fences on the funny farm. Have any bizarre thoughts? Welcome to the party. What music are you playing?

Excuse me, but I have to stop now.

My doorbell just rang.

It might be the Village People.

76

Zoo Story

Once upon a time, far away, but not so long ago, a woman gave me three wishes. I was not surprised. I think of her as a fairy godmother because much of what she does has a quality of magic about it. She gave me the wishes on a Sunday morning, in the city of Prague, in the Czech Republic.

Placing three carefully folded pieces of yellow paper in the palm of my hand, she said, "Choose one. That will tell us where to go today."

The one I picked said, "To the Zoo."

Wonderful! We went.

The Prague Zoo is unique because in 2001 a great flood washed much of it away. Many animals were lost, or died, or escaped. It's not your usual zoo. But there's a new beginning, constructed around the survivors. Many of the new facilities still have no animals in them.

"Don't worry," said my fairy godmother. "There will be animals. We will imagine them." And that's how I saw a saber-tooth tiger, a mastodon, a unicorn, a satyr, and a dragon. Also my first pterodactyl.

That evening, when I was emptying out my pockets, I found the other two wishes. I opened the first one. "To the Zoo," it said.

And you've already guessed the third wish.

Yes. "To the Zoo."

Fairy Godmothers play by their own rules.

Otherwise I would never have seen all the animals.

77

The Names That Remain

My task for the next two days: Organize my address books—bring order out of the chaos of names and numbers. I was going to do this last year. And the year before that. Not having a cell phone, not owning a Blackberry, and not using a computer except to write words, means holding onto data with cryptic pencil-scribbling in little black books and inserting little scraps of paper and business cards until I have a fat paper sandwich, not an address book. Not even a rubber band holds it flat now. Time to clean house.

In reviewing this mess I am reminded how much of my life is lived relating to a passing procession of people who come and go by happenstance, not design. Neighbors, business colleagues, fellow travelers, members of clubs, and tradesmen.

Some names are mysterious—*Who is this? Why are they here?* I ask myself. So many of these names can be crossed off—actors on the stage of one's life who have a few lines, play a small part, and go offstage never to return.

Also noted is the restlessness of my friends and acquaintances for many of whom I have a long string of changing numbers and addresses—along with additions of cell and fax numbers and e-mail addresses, making an indecipherable chaos of my little black book. (What will be added next? Personal global positioning satellite coordinates?)

I will not throw the used books away, a decision inspired by a friend who thinks of his little black books as personal history. He has eight of his from as far back as his college days. Once in a while he reads through them. He says I take up several pages in his book because I'm such a transient.

I wonder how many other places my name and numbers are recorded? And I wonder if there are those who will review their books and files this year, find my name, and eliminate it as no longer being on their stage in their play: "Forget him, whoever he was . . ."

And I wonder about those whose names will never appear in my records because I just missed meeting them by not being at the same dinner, by living a block away instead of next door, or by not being at a parent's meeting or by changing plane or train reservations or whatever ad infinitum.

The friends who might have been but never were.

I miss some of them.

I wonder if they miss me?

And there is that everlasting mystery: This man on page 9 is my long-time good friend, and this other man on page 12 is my long-time good friend, but they don't particularly care for each other and probably aren't in each other's little black books. Odd.

Thanks to the plus side of life's friendship lottery, there are those whose names have been in my book for years beyond remembering. Their many numbers may change, but they remain to play primary roles in my life year after year, wherever they are. Not so many names, really. And less, as age and disability and death remove them from the active list.

These are the names I know by heart, whose telephone numbers are stored in the meat of my mind, whose images are not digital but mental. I know who they are and where they are and why they are there. When I triage my little black book and begin a new one, I will write their names and numbers first—mostly from memory going back as far as fifty years.

These are the Essential Friends. The Companions of a Lifetime. Those I can call in the middle of the night, anytime, anywhere. In sorrow or in joy. We know each other so well we need not identify ourselves—we know the sound of the voice on the phone from the first word. The conversation does not begin from scratch—it is ongoing. One special friend—a pianist—plays music as his way of greeting. I always know it's him.

And now, as time takes its toll, these are the voices that will speak over graves in the end. We don't know which voices will give whose eulogy, but we know we are keepers of each other's history and witnesses to each other's lives. We will be there, one way or another. And whoever has the last word will not leave out the joy of the laughter or the songs or the jokes.

The updating of my little black book goes slowly. I don't mind. I review these names, connect them to memories, and get lost in nostalgia. The names that remain remind me that I am a rich and lucky man. And not nearly as alone as I sometimes fear that I am.

78

Brick

This is a note to accompany the gift of a brick to an old friend. It is not a poem—just a one-line-at-a time expression of grace.

Here is a common red brick,
Found on a small beach on Seattle's Elliot Bay,
At 6:45 in the morning on the fifteenth day of July,
At the beginning of an elegant day in high summer.
Clear skies, calm sea, low tide, and sixty degrees.
A green Chinese cargo container ship coasted by,
outward bound for the deep blue sea.
This brick was half in and half out of the water,
covered and uncovered by the rising and falling of the tide.
The brick is made from iron-rich clay, eons old,
ground down and left behind by glaciers from Canada,
reclaimed from the earth, I know not how or where.

Mixed with water, molded, fired,
brought to a building site and placed in a wall,
where it steadfastly served its purpose for some long time,
until the building was demolished into rubble and
dumped on the waterfront as fill to make a park.
The working waves of the salt sea sorted out the brick,
leaving it for me to find and rescue.
I washed off the seaweed and sand,
and brought the brick home, where it has been sitting
on my desk, keeping me company, provoking my mind.
This brick is old and weathered, yet solid still.
It could be used again as the first brick in some new
construction.
Or employed, less nobly, as a doorstop.
Or perhaps it could serve as the First Stone
To throw at someone more guilty than I.
It might be seen as a unique and essential thing:
Made of earth and water and fire and stardust and time . . .
Perhaps containing spirits by now.
Could it speak, it would have great stories to tell.
Sometimes I imagine it to be the wrapping for an
Image of the Buddha. An image to be freed
By the eye of a sculptor.
Someone with vision. Like you.
This brick is a small monument to possibility.
Compost waiting to be made useful by imagination.
The worthless that could become priceless.

I tell you all this, because
I was thinking about you when I found the brick.
And wishing you were there with me on that fine morning.
This brick has a history.
It has been through a lot.
As we have.
The brick is still strong and will last a long time.
As our friendship will.
I thought you might like to have it.
You, whose steadfastness always makes me say,
"You're a real brick."

79

How to Paddle
a Canoe . . . or a Life

There is a twelve-inch wooden ruler in the top drawer of my desk. The ruler has been mine since the first week in September 1947. The facts are certain because, in barely legible penciled letters on the back are these words: *"Bobby Fulghum, Fifth Grade, Sanger Avenue Elementary School."*

The ruler is one of those rare artifacts that have survived the triage of my possessions over sixty years. It remains as useful now as it was then. And it reminds me now of the delicious childhood pleasure of shopping for school supplies before classes began each September.

The right tools always promised a fine school year. Yellow pencils, lined notebook paper and ring binder, pencil sharpener, eraser, books, and workbooks. And brown paper covers to be carefully folded around those books. And a new metal lunch box.

Equipped. Ready. Confident.

Alas, along with the supplies came the annual review of my report cards from the previous year. My father's job. The "You-could-do-better" talk. And by fifth grade it was clear that doing better involved mathematics.

Not so confident.

Somewhere along the way of my early years in school the fog of number phobia had risen in the swampy edges of my mind. The multiplying and dividing of fractions seemed more a matter of faith than fact, and while I had learned to fake it, I could not really do it. Too proud to admit incompetence, I promised to do better. I meant to do better. But I never did.

Now I know that if I had only asked for help, a very little more information and encouragement would have filled what has ever after been a permanent pothole in my self-image.

Math inadequacy wasn't really the problem.

An unwillingness to ask for help was.

This memory came to mind when I took a long walk on Labor Day afternoon out through the wetlands area in Seattle's arboretum. I watched as canoes came from the rental dock across the channel to negotiate the entrance to the inner waterways. They had to pass under the small bridge on which I was standing. Most of the canoes carried a family—mother in the bow, children amidships, and father in the stern. As the first canoe approached, I sensed calamity.

The boaters' incompetence was obvious. Instead of forging ahead in a straight line, the canoe made long erratic zigzags as the paddlers frantically switched sides to compensate for the canoe's bizarre behavior. By the time they reached the bridge, frustration had become anger, as mother and father both tried to take command of the helm of the canoe.

"Godammit, Martha, stop what you're doing."

"Godammit, Charley, you don't know what you're doing."

"Yes I do. I did this at summer camp."

"Well, you didn't learn a thing."

"Left!"

"No, right!"

"Left, Left, LEFT!"

"Don't yell at me!"

"Then stop telling me what to do!"

"Backpaddle, backpaddle! BACKPADDLE!"

"Watch out!"

And they managed to hit the bridge piling dead on.

"You stupidsonofabitch!"

"Don't call me that!"

"You are stupid! It's all your fault!"

Their two little girls began bawling—they wanted to go home—now. And the parents, defeated, sat fuming, sloshing back and forth in the gentle waves of the lake on a lovely, sunny Labor Day, as other family canoes-in-crisis begin piling up behind them, even banging into them.

Happy holiday.

Meanwhile, two other canoes came swiftly across the channel and passed skillfully under the bridge. A third slowed and asked the demoralized flotilla if they needed any help.

"Oh, no. Oh, no, we'll get the hang of it."

Even I, an experienced canoeist, offered advice.

"Oh, no. Oh, no. We'll be just fine."

If they had only been willing to ask me, such a small amount of information would have made such a big difference. I would have said:

"The bow paddler is only an engine, paddling straight ahead.

The stern paddler is the captain and makes all decisions in simple terms: Paddle, stop paddling, switch sides, back paddle.

The stern controls direction by paddling with a J-stroke—back and out—or using the paddle as a rudder.

The passengers sit still in the middle.

Nobody stands up. That's it. Why do it the hard way?"

Ask somebody? Ha! Never!

Today I am about to go out and repair my outboard motor. I know who knows how to do it. But I'm as smart as he is. *Right.* I can do it myself. *Right.* How hard can this be? *Right. Ask somebody? Ha! Never!*

But his motor works. Mine does not.

(Pause.)

The voice of my father echoes out of the backroom of my mind—the old mantra: "Could do better." So, bygod, I will go down the dock and talk to my neighborly expert. Finally admitting ignorance, I may finally learn something useful. This could establish a trend! This could be my year to finally do better! And who knows? Maybe the outboard motor genius could teach me about dividing fractions while he's at it. I'll ask.

When the student is finally ready, the teacher appears.

80

Blessing

In Switzerland there is a city. Geneva. A river flows through it. In that river is an island. On that island is a restaurant. And in that restaurant is a man. Me. Looking out a window at a stormy day. The eleventh day of October in 2006.

Outside, tall plane trees are being thrashed by a blustery wind. Their dry yellow leaves are launched out onto the Rhone River as it races by on its way to the sea at Marseilles. The leaves float like a brave regatta of tiny sailboats, floating and whirling in unison. The rain fills them, sinking them into the current of the river.

Evanescence is the word that comes to mind—the inevitable brevity of the beauty in life. If I were Japanese, I would write a *haiku* about this moment.

———

In the room where I stand are three long tables, well set for a fine lunch. White linen, crystal glasses, silverware, and roses. Just sitting down together are thirty people gathered for a meal before attending an afternoon awards ceremony to honor two defenders of human rights.

As the guests settle into place, I consider them.

There, at that table, is Arnold Tsunga, a black African lawyer from Zimbabwe who gave up his private life and practice to work for those who are wrongly arrested, tortured, and imprisoned. He himself was beaten and tortured. He will be honored today.

And there, at that table is Akbar Ganji, a journalist from Iran, who was arrested and tortured and imprisoned for daring to speak his mind and criticize his government. He will be honored today.

Sitting around them are friends, colleagues, and fellow activists. There, a woman from the International Red Cross; there, a man from the United Nations High Commission for Refugees; there a woman from Amnesty International; here, a man who has worked in nine countries for five agencies committed to helping those who cannot help themselves.

My eye moves on from face to face, recognizing those who have made it their life's work to defend human rights, and to work for justice and peace in the world, at the sacrifice of their own wellbeing. If you passed them in the streets of Geneva, you would not know. If you could see into their hearts and minds you would never forget the fire that is there.

It's so very important to know that such people are real. They exist.

They are part of our world.

My thoughts are interrupted by the master of cere- monies, calling my name, saying that, since I am an or- dained minister, I will offer a blessing for the meal. In deference to universal religious custom, the guests begin to bow their heads.

"Wait," I say.

"This blessing does not require you to close your eyes or bow your heads. I ask that you keep your eyes open, your heads up.

Listen.

The finest blessing a meal can have is great compan- ionship.

Look around this room. Take notice of those who sit with you.

Look around you. Look at these men and women.

Consider who they are, what they have done, and what they stand for.

Consider that you are not alone on your Way in the world.

Consider that you have the honor to break bread with such as these.

Look.

And know that this meal and each of us is abundantly blessed.

Amen."

I pass this blessing on to you. That you, too, may know that, despite the evanescence of life, such people are still hard at work in the world. You may even be one of them.

I pass this blessing on to you. That you, too, may keep your eyes open and your head up. That you, too, may see and know and act. That you, too, may bless and be blessed.

8 1

The Meaning of Life

*This essay was written many years ago, and first ap-
peared in my second book. In time I came to live where
the story began, in close contact with the man the story belongs to. With better information the essay has been revised
for accuracy. The spirit of the story of the mirror remains
unchanged and bears repeating. Though set in Crete, it's
about a universal premise.*

"Are there any questions?"

A standard offer at the end of lectures and long meetings.

The ritual gesture is meant to indicate openness on the
part of the speaker, but if in fact you do ask a question,
both the speaker and the audience will probably give you
drop-dead looks. Still, there always seems to be some

earnest dimwit who has a question. And the speaker usually answers—repeating most of what he has already said.

When there actually is some time left and there is silence in response to the invitation, I often ask the most important question of all:

"What is the meaning of life?"

What? Why? Well, you never know—somebody may have a good answer, and I'd really hate to miss it, because I was too socially inhibited to ask. Once, and only once, I got a serious answer to my question.

An answer that is with me still.

First, I must tell you where this happened, because the place has a power of its own. Near the village of Kolymbari, on a rocky bay of the island of Crete, stands a Greek Orthodox monastery. Alongside it, on land donated by the monastery, is an institute dedicated to human understanding and peace, with a special mission to achieve rapprochement between Germans and Cretans. An improbable task, given the bitter residue of World War II.

This site is important, because it overlooks the small airstrip at Maleme across the bay where Nazi paratroopers invaded Crete. During the invasion they were attacked by ordinary Cretans with antique guns, kitchen knives, pitchforks, and hay scythes. The German retribution was terrible. The populations of whole villages were lined up and shot for assaulting Hitler's finest troops. High above the institute is a memorial with a single cross marking the mass grave of young Greek men killed in the fight around the monastery. In all the surrounding villages there are graves of those men and women and children who died fighting the Germans. Not soldiers—citizens. Every village square has its monument to those who died.

And across the bay, on the hill above the airstrip, is the regimented burial ground of the Nazi paratroopers. The memorials are so placed that all might see and never forget. Hate was the only weapon the Cretans had at the end, and it was a weapon many vowed never to give up. Never. Ever.

Against this heavy curtain of history, in this place where the stone of hatred is hard and thick, the existence of an institute devoted to healing the wounds of war is a fragile paradox. The Orthodox Academy of Crete.

How has it come to be here?

The answer is a man. Alexander Papaderos.

A doctor of philosophy, teacher, politician, citizen of

the world, but a son of this soil. After the war he went to Germany for his graduate education. He came to believe that the Germans and the Cretans had much to give one another—much to learn from one another. Moreover, they had an example to set. If they could forgive each other and construct a creative relationship, then any people could.

To make a fine story short, with the support of the legendary Bishop Ireinaios, Papaderos succeeded. The institute became a reality—a conference ground on the site of horror—and it did indeed become a source of productive interaction between the two countries. Books could be written on the dreams that were realized by what people gave to people in this place. Now, from all over the world, groups come to address conflict and to exchange the ideas that bring people together instead of dividing them.

Alexander Papaderos: One look at him and you understood—saw his strength and intensity. Energy, physical power, courage, intelligence, passion, and vivacity radiated from his person. And to speak to him, to shake his hand, to be in a room with him when he spoke, was to experience his extraordinary humanity. Few men live up to their reputations when you get close. Alexander Papaderos was an exception.

At the last session on the last morning of a two-week seminar on Greek culture, led by intellectuals and experts in their fields who were recruited by Papaderos from across Greece, he rose from his chair at the back of the room and walked to the front, where he stood in the bright Greek sunlight of an open window and looked out. He turned. And made the ritual gesture: "Are there any questions?"

Silence. These two weeks had generated enough questions for a lifetime, but for now there was only mute stillness.

"No questions?" Papaderos swept the room with his eyes.

So. I asked.

"Dr. Papaderos, what is the meaning of life?"

Uneasy laughter followed, and people stirred to go.

Papaderos held up his hand and stilled the room. He looked at me for a long time, asking with his eyes if I was serious, and seeing, from my eyes that, yes, I was.

"I will answer your question."

Taking his wallet out of his hip pocket, he fished into a leather billfold and brought out a very small round mirror, about the size of a quarter. He turned the mirror over in his fingers, and began talking in a quiet, reflective voice.

"When I was a small child, during the war, we were very poor and we lived in a remote mountain village. One day, on the road, I found the broken pieces of a mirror. A German motorcycle had been wrecked in that place.

"I tried to find all the pieces of the mirror and put them together, but it was not possible, so I kept only the largest piece. This one. And by scratching it on a stone I made it round. I began to play with it as a toy and became fascinated by the fact that I could reflect light into dark places where the sun would never shine—in deep holes and crevices and dark closets and behind walls. It became a game for me to get light into the most inaccessible places I could find.

"I kept the little mirror, and as I went about my growing up, I would take it out in idle moments and continue the challenge of the game. As I became a man, I grew to understand that this was not just child's play but a metaphor for what I might do with my life. I came to understand that I am not the light or the source of light. But light— the light of truth, understanding, and knowledge—is there, and that light will only shine in many dark places if I reflect it.

"I am a fragment of a mirror whose whole design and shape I do not know. Nevertheless, with what I have I can reflect light into the dark places of this world—into the dreary places in the hearts of men—and change some things in some people. Perhaps others may see and do likewise. This is what I am about. This is the meaning of my life."

And then he took his small mirror and, holding it carefully, caught the bright rays of daylight streaming through the window and reflected them onto my face and onto my hands folded on the desk.

Much of what I experienced in the way of information about Greek culture and history that summer is gone from memory. But in the wallet of my mind I carry a small round mirror still.

I know what I can do with it.

And what I can do with me.

Are there any questions?

You might like to know that this story has a life of its own now, traveling around the world, passed on as a treasure by those who read it. I wish to keep it moving by this retelling. A part of the story is close by me as I write this. One Christmas, Dr. Papaderos gave me a small velvet pouch. "Keep this for me," he said. Inside was the mirror.

82

The Way of Water

From its inception, the purpose of the Orthodox Academy of Crete was postwar reconciliation between people and cultures and ideas. Simple: Bring intelligent people together—something good might happen. But progress was often hard and slow and frustrating against the headwinds of lasting antagonism. Still, surprising breakthroughs were often made. And the accomplishments of the Academy were not always achieved in solemn convocations.

There are other ways.

Cretan humor and cleverness played their part.

I will tell you a story—of three minor miracles.

One of the earliest conferences held at the OAC involved fairly high-level politicians from France, Germany, and Greece. They and their spouses arrived with serious attitudes—wearing serious clothes—as if prepared for a serious court hearing instead of dialogue. Unresolved feelings of mistrust hung like curtains between them at the reception and the first meeting. The national groups did not even mix and mingle informally at the first dinner.

A tense affair.

The Executive Director of the Academy, Dr. Papaderos, was vexed by the unproductive atmosphere. What to do?

And then a strange thing happened. During the night, somehow, the water system failed. Strange, because the Academy's facilities were new—all the utilities functioned well.

At breakfast Dr. Papaderos declared the problem and said the only solution was to organize a bucket brigade from the spring at the nearby monastery to bring water to the Academy's storage tank so that all might drink, and flush toilets, and wash. The participants would have to do the work until the problem was fixed. Were they willing?

Well . . . well . . . OK.

Thus in the hot Cretan summer sun, the French and Germans and Greeks, in shorts and bathing suits, began hauling water. As they became tired and sweaty, the inevitable happened. The French began splashing water on each other. The Germans and Greeks joined in. Suddenly whole buckets of water were being thrown, and it was not long before an all-out water war was going on in the road between the Academy and the monastery.

Nobody was exempt—not even the monks or the Academy staff or Dr. Papaderos. Nationality was forgotten in the good-humored melee. Playful chaos prevailed. And, best of all, there was laughter.

A minor miracle.

A supply of cold beer appeared. The second minor miracle.

And sopping wet, tipsy on beer, and united in the great fun of a water war, the conference was at last ready for serious business. It went on to fine accomplishments in a spirit of lasting reconciliation.

The third miracle: Water at the Academy was restored that night.

Though Dr. Papaderos only smiles to this day when asked about the miracles, everybody guessed who turned the water off and who turned it on and why.

This story reminds me of lines from the Tao te Ching:

Nothing in the world
Is as soft and yielding as water.
Yet for dissolving the hard and the inflexible,
Nothing can surpass it.
The soft overcomes the hard;
The gentle overcomes the rigid.

Everyone knows this is true,
But few can put it into practice.

I know at least one man who knows how to put this wisdom into practice. I pass him every day in the halls of the Academy.

He knows why I sometimes smile at him. He is a clever man.

It makes me a little nervous sometimes when he smiles at me.

When I arrived in Crete this year, the plumbing in my house was backed up. Cleaning out the drains was a dirty, humbling task, but I did it. My accomplishment gave me a new relationship with the maintenance staff of the Academy. Dr. Papaderos seemed pleased. He smiled at me when I told him what I'd done.

I do wonder how the drains got stopped up in the first place.

He wouldn't . . . ?

83

Intersection:
Writing the Life

A Greek journalist asked me, "Do you follow a set of principles about your writing?" Well . . . yes and no.

I tend to dodge and weave when asked to explain about the writing process. I don't think I have any wisdom to add to the abundance of books and courses about writing. But the truth is that I do puzzle over why and how I write. And I have addressed three memos to myself about what I do. The memos are posted prominently on the wall of the studio where I work—in the space where I sort ideas at the beginning of a writing project.

Over time, the memos have been reconsidered, expanded, and revised, because I actively consult them. They are included here at the suggestion of friends who browse the scrapbook accumulated on my walls.

"Might be useful," they say.

The memos are at the least windows opening into the workshop of my mind when I am Writing the Life.

Have a look.

84

Unfinished Manifesto

Creative writing is an art.

Being an artist is a way of life, not a job.

Do not write to make a living; write to make living
worthwhile.

Write to make sense of my life and then pass that along.

Write from having lived as wide, as deep, and as varied a
life as possible. Specialization is for insects.

Use both solitude and company. And remember that it is
just as easy to fail at solitude as it is to fail at being a
companion.

Creative writing is a moral, social act. Don't lose sight
of that.

Justice, mercy, love, and freedom are not the work of the
gods or politicians, but the work of those who willingly
risk seeing the world with open eyes—who do not turn
away, but address what they see.

Good ought to be—evil ought not to be—and you can't be
an artist if you don't know which is which and on what
side you must come down.

An artist should strive to be useful.

85

Voluntary Exile

A second sheet of paper is posted alongside the Unfin-ished Manifesto. In order to concentrate on writing I usually shut myself away in Utah or in Crete, or take long solitary journeys where I can be reached only with difficulty. My self-admonitions for such times are these:

Go on. Escape over the walls of your asylum.
Go slowly. On the side of your cart, write UNWARD!
Pull the cart yourself.
Collect kindling for your fire as you go,
But expect spontaneous combustion.
Live in the tent of the invisible traveler.
Abandon irony; cage ennui; shrug off the pale clothes of
    the mundane.
Nail angst to the floor and stomp it flat.
Set aside the dead brick of certainty.
Eat the bread of uncertainty for lunch.

Carry the wine of carelessness and drink deep.

Sing. Dance. You are the only audience who cares how
   well.

Look through the lens of passion and joy.

Be a-mused—the muse that laughs.

Always ask the next question.

Always take the long way around.

Always turn back two blocks short of the abyss.

Go on. You may.

Be as many people as need be.

Never go back the way you came.

Go on. Do it yourself.

Go on. Never quit.

Go on. Never finish.

Go on. Flourish.

86

Instructions for Wayfarers

 This last memo is a permission slip—from me for me:

They will tell you: All the trips have been taken.
You will say: I have not been to see for myself.
They will insist: Everything has already been said.
You will insist: I have not had my say.
They will tell you: It's all been done.
You will reply: My way is not finished.
But be warned: Any way is long—and any way is hard.
Fear not.
You are the gate.
You are the gatekeeper.
You may go through and on and on.
And fare you well.

87

Meanwhile

Some sense of being successful in life may lie in knowing which league to play in. If you are and have always been short, chubby, and slow, and your sense of success means playing striker on a World Cup soccer team, failure will be your lot in life.

Wrong league.

However, if you are pleased to play goalie on a local playground team with other short, chubby, and slow people—and you have a wonderful time doing it, then you are a successful soccer player.

Right league.

And the same is true for any sport—tennis, baseball, volleyball, poker or whatever—pick a league worthy of your abilities and flourish there.

Or, as Epictetus said in the first century BC: *"If you can fish, fish. If you can sing, sing. If you can fight, fight. Determine what you can do. And do that."*

Likewise, some sense of being successful in life may lie in knowing on which scale you work best. For example, an astronomer is one whose mind can work on a cosmic scale. A physicist is one whose mind can handle the quantum scale. A theologian—the metaphysical scale. A historian deals with the long picture. A psychiatrist works with the deep picture. A cook or taxi driver attends the immediate situation. Poets and artists operate on a very personal scale.

Many people die confused and unfulfilled, because they spend a life trying to perform above or even below their abilities and perspective—usually a matter of working on the wrong scale.

Epictetus said, *"Why worry about being a nobody when what matters is being a somebody in those areas of your life over which you have control, and in which you can make a difference?"*

Why am I telling you this?

When I arrived in Crete this year I found on my desk a letter addressed to me from a German scholar who had lived in my house for a time while I was away. She has read my books and reads my Web site journal postings.

After expressing appreciation for my writing and the use of the house, she asked some hard questions:

Why did I not address the political issues of our time, especially the actions of the present American government
administration? Why did I not address the humanitarian issues of our day? Why was I not outraged as an American
with the evil done on my behalf? Did I agree that might
makes right, that the end justifies the means, and that God
is on our side? How can I support the fundamental position
of Zionist Israel? Did I really believe the American Way was
the only Way? Did I have any real understanding of how
America is perceived in the world now? How much hatred
and contempt is felt? Why was I silent on these burning issues? Why did I not run for office and do something?

Answer: It is a matter of league and scale.

My mind works on the scale of the local, the daily, and the
    ordinary.
Writing about that is the league in which I am competent.
I tend to be simple-minded, plain-spoken, and optimistic.
I attend to my corner of the world as best I can with the
    tools I have.

Of course evil and ugliness exists, as much now as ever.
These get all the headlines. We all know about the bad news.
Plenty reasons for pessimism. The wrongs of the world are
    clear.
I'm as outraged and frustrated as most of us are.

And I send money and vote and sometimes march in
protest.

Still, we shall all die. The climate will change. The seas
will rise.

The glaciers will be back. Life will evolve in unimagined
forms.

And, finally, the Earth will fall into the sun.

That's the truth.

But for the time being, there's what I call The Meanwhile
Factor.

Meanwhile, I remain astonished at the good and lovely that
exists.

And most of it is free and readily available if I'll look for it.

Meanwhile . . . is the league and scale of the amateurs
like me.

I do not have the skill to play professional sports.

Wrong league.

I do not have the competence to be an astrologer,
physicist, theologian, chef, historian, politician,
psychiatrist, cook, or taxi driver.

Wrong scale.

Neither the talent to be a poet, musician, or artist. Nor
writer of great literature or even thrillers or detective
stories or political commentary.

Wrong ambition.

I am a storyteller at heart. I am a man who goes about
trying to be awake to the news of the immediate ordinary

world; to make sense of what I see; to pass my thoughts along. I try to answer the Great Mother Questions. I ask, out of amused confusion, "What is going on?" and "Have you noticed?"

And I say, in one way or another, "Meanwhile, don't miss the good stuff. Pass it on." If I have a message, that's pretty much it.

There. Not a self-defense or an apology.

Just a statement of position.

The world and the universe go their inevitable way.

Meanwhile . . . I know what I can do.

Meanwhile . . . I do it.

The Essays